brilliant

how to be a brilliant leader

how to be a brilliant leader

Second edition

Simon Cooper

PEARSON

Harlow, England • London • New York • Boston • San Francisco • Toronto • Sydney • Auckland • Singapore • Hong Kong
Tokyo • Seoul • Taipei • New Delhi • Cape Town • São Paulo • Mexico City • Madrid • Amsterdam • Munich • Paris • Milan

PEARSON EDUCATION LIMITED

Edinburgh Gate
Harlow CM20 2JE
United Kingdom
Tel: +44 (0)1279 623623
Web: www.pearson.com/uk

First published as *Brilliant Leader* 2008, 2010 (print and electronic)
Second edition published as *Brilliant Leader* 2011, 2012 (print and electronic)
Rejacketed edition 2015 (print and electronic)

ISBN: 978-1-292-08105-2 (print)
       978-1-292-08444-2 (PDF)
       978-1-292-08445-9 (eText)
       978-1-292-08456-5 (ePub)

British Library Cataloguing-in-Publication Data
A catalogue record for the print edition is available from the British Library

Library of Congress Cataloging-in-Publication Data
A catalog record for the print edition is available from the Library of Congress

10 9 8 7 6 5 4 3 2 1
18 17 16 15 14

Series cover design by David Carroll & Co

Print edition typeset in 10/14pt Plantin MT Pro by 71
Print edition printed and bound in Great Britain by Henry Ling Ltd, at the Dorset
Press, Dorchester, Dorset

NOTE THAT ANY PAGE CROSS REFERENCES REFER TO THE PRINT EDITION

For Sara, without your love and support I would be but half the man that I have become

Foreword

American-born British retailer Harry Gordon Selfridge said:

The boss drives people; the leader coaches them. The boss depends on authority; the leader on goodwill. The boss inspires fear; the leader inspires enthusiasm. The boss says 'I'; the leader says 'WE'. The boss fixes the blame for the breakdown; the leader fixes the breakdown. The boss says 'GO'; the leader says 'LET'S GO!'

I think of Selfridge's quote often when Simon Cooper and I are training leaders and managers in the workshops we occasionally run together. Selfridge captures an aspect of leadership that is as relevant today as it was when he was leading at Marshall Fields and later when he opened his own store in London: bosses care about *what* gets done; leaders care about *how* things get done.

Imagine how far before his time Selfridge was when he focused on the way leaders led back at the turn of the twentieth century. He had an insight many of the leaders I meet today have not yet learned: coaching, goodwill, enthusiasm, teamwork, action-orientation and shared leadership are the alchemy that separates a brilliant leader from an average one. How did Selfridge come to this so early, before much of the seminal research had been done about leadership and motivation? Perhaps I found the answer in another quote of his. Selfridge was thinking about why people buy when he said, 'People will sit up and take notice of you, if you will sit up and take notice of what makes them sit up and take notice.' This idea led him to a number of firsts in the world of retail. Yet it also contains another keen observation about brilliant leadership – great leaders connect with people in highly empathic ways. If you want to lead in ways that impact results, you need to connect with people and their motivations. You need to adapt your style to suit the situation you find yourself in and the ways the people around you want to be led.

The goal of every brilliant leader is to create connections that go beyond the work or the job to leverage willingness, loyalty and commitment. This is what Selfridge alludes to when he speaks about 'I' versus 'we' and 'go' versus 'let's go'. A brilliant leader enlists co-workers to put their heart into their work, along with their head, and to approach work from a place of commitment and connection. Saying 'let's go' encourages co-workers to actively engage in doing what needs to be done, improving processes, measuring results and seeking continuous improvement. Brilliant leaders use influence not only to serve the current situation, but also to build capacity and capability for the future of the enterprise. They envision a future they can reach with their teams. 'Let's go' is the beginning of a journey made together to a shared, preferable future. With goodwill and enthusiasm as fuel and a clear vision of the destination, a brilliant leader moves a team forward. The alchemy of brilliant leadership is that once the leader communicates the destination, the team makes progress towards it magnetically – making all the right moves along the way. And they do it while needing less and less direction over time.

Being a leader is a big job – embarking on the mission of becoming a brilliant one can be daunting. When Simon and I begin our management training workshops we ask the groups we are working with to list the attributes of a great leader. In a short time we are turning the fifth, sixth then seventh flipchart page. There can easily be 60 or 70 attributes on the massive list describing an effective leader (not even a brilliant one!). The group ends this discussion by asking, 'Of all of these attributes,

Contents

About the author

Simon Cooper has over 25 years' experience of building, developing and leading high-performance teams.

His early career was in the finance industry where he primarily built and led several successful sales teams. Following this, Simon moved to the recruitment sector where he built up and ran a series of regional offices, incorporating front line sales teams and back office support teams, before being appointed Managing Director.

When the business was sold some two years later, Simon became an independent consultant specialising in leadership and business skills development. Over the past 10 years he has helped to develop thousands of leaders within hundreds of organisations worldwide via seminars, workshops, coaching and experiential events.

Simon currently works in organisation effectiveness for Informatica Corporation, driving strategic change and developing leaders worldwide.

Contact: scooper@informatica.com

Foreword

American-born British retailer Harry Gordon Selfridge said:

The boss drives people; the leader coaches them. The boss depends on authority; the leader on goodwill. The boss inspires fear; the leader inspires enthusiasm. The boss says 'I'; the leader says 'WE'. The boss fixes the blame for the breakdown; the leader fixes the breakdown. The boss says 'GO'; the leader says 'LET'S GO!'

I think of Selfridge's quote often when Simon Cooper and I are training leaders and managers in the workshops we occasionally run together. Selfridge captures an aspect of leadership that is as relevant today as it was when he was leading at Marshall Fields and later when he opened his own store in London: bosses care about *what* gets done; leaders care about *how* things get done.

Imagine how far before his time Selfridge was when he focused on the way leaders led back at the turn of the twentieth century. He had an insight many of the leaders I meet today have not yet learned: coaching, goodwill, enthusiasm, teamwork, action-orientation and shared leadership are the alchemy that separates a brilliant leader from an average one. How did Selfridge come to this so early, before much of the seminal research had been done about leadership and motivation? Perhaps I found the answer in another quote of his. Selfridge was thinking about why people buy when he said, 'People will sit up and take notice of you, if you will sit up and take notice of what makes them sit up and take notice.' This idea led him to a number of firsts in the world of retail. Yet it also contains another keen observation about brilliant leadership – great leaders connect with people in highly empathic ways. If you want to lead in ways that impact results, you need to connect with people and their motivations. You need to adapt your style to suit the situation you find yourself in and the ways the people around you want to be led.

The goal of every brilliant leader is to create connections that go beyond the work or the job to leverage willingness, loyalty and commitment. This is what Selfridge alludes to when he speaks about 'I' versus 'we' and 'go' versus 'let's go'. A brilliant leader enlists co-workers to put their heart into their work, along with their head, and to approach work from a place of commitment and connection. Saying 'let's go' encourages co-workers to actively engage in doing what needs to be done, improving processes, measuring results and seeking continuous improvement. Brilliant leaders use influence not only to serve the current situation, but also to build capacity and capability for the future of the enterprise. They envision a future they can reach with their teams. 'Let's go' is the beginning of a journey made together to a shared, preferable future. With goodwill and enthusiasm as fuel and a clear vision of the destination, a brilliant leader moves a team forward. The alchemy of brilliant leadership is that once the leader communicates the destination, the team makes progress towards it magnetically – making all the right moves along the way. And they do it while needing less and less direction over time.

Being a leader is a big job – embarking on the mission of becoming a brilliant one can be daunting. When Simon and I begin our management training workshops we ask the groups we are working with to list the attributes of a great leader. In a short time we are turning the fifth, sixth then seventh flipchart page. There can easily be 60 or 70 attributes on the massive list describing an effective leader (not even a brilliant one!). The group ends this discussion by asking, 'Of all of these attributes, which is the most important?' The answer: all of them. Managing is a balancing act or, more pointedly, a juggling act. Brilliant managers know what to use their energy on and what they can skip. They play to their strengths and the strengths of their team. Being a brilliant leader is dancing like Ginger Rogers – doing everything Fred Astaire did, only backwards and in high heels.

Which is why I am pleased Simon has written a book that focuses on the dimensions of brilliant leadership in the way Harry Selfridge would have. It focuses on the human side of managing – hiring the best people, communicating with them, ensuring their growth, meeting their needs yet doing it all while things change at a speed Selfridge never could have anticipated. While I am sure that there is no single right way to manage, I am also sure that brilliant managing is not about doing: it is about being. Selfridge knew that too, so, rather than the right way, he focused on the right intention. Read the helpful advice in Simon's book and combine it with Selfridge's insight of 'we' not 'I', and 'let's go', rather than 'go'. Together, they form the blueprint for becoming a brilliant leader!

Jason Ollander-Krane
Organisation Effectiveness Informatica Corporation

Introduction

Leadership is about creating an environment where people consistently perform to the best of their ability. Natural leaders do this intuitively, but, for the rest of us mere mortals, we have to learn how to lead. In this book my aim is to give you a framework and a set of principles that will help you to lead others to consistently deliver high levels of performance.

What makes a brilliant leader?

I guess this is the million dollar question. To be a brilliant leader you need to be many things. You need to be a chameleon, adapting your style as and when the needs of your people and the situation dictate. Brilliant leaders do this instinctively so you will need to hone your instinct in this area.

Brilliant leaders also tend to be great communicators. This is how you build rapport with your team members, communicate your vision, your expectations and provide feedback on progress. However, brilliant leaders are also results focused and objective. There is little room for sentiment and, ultimately, you will be judged on your team's performance – you have to deliver results through the efforts of others and to do this you must create an environment in which your people can perform at a high level.

You can only consistently deliver results through others if you have their respect and they are prepared to follow where you lead them. This, then, is a key difference between management and leadership. Managers tend to use **position power** to get the job done – that is, 'I am your manager, do what I say.' Brilliant leaders will only use position power as a last resort; their first option is to use **respect power**. That is, the creation of an environment where people both want to and can perform at their optimum.

Respect, of course, must be earned – only poor managers think it is a rite of passage. The advice and guidance in the following chapters will help you earn the respect required to get the job done, consistently and to a high standard. These principles and techniques will also help you do so in a manner that maximises staff commitment and loyalty.

> respect, of course, must be earned

Management and leadership – what's the difference?

If you run an internet search on that question you will get a whole host of different opinions and ideas. The most compelling argument I have heard is that all leaders can manage, but not all managers can lead. This implies that there is something extra about leadership. Take a look at this example.

A staff member resists a task that they don't like doing, such as monthly statistics. The options open to the leader or manager in this situation are as follows.

1 Tell them to do it – no arguments.

2 Get someone else to do it instead.

3 Get them to do it diligently and willingly.

Options 1 and 2 are both management actions whereas option 3 is a leadership outcome.

The purpose of this book is to help you explore the 'something extra' that makes for great leadership and help you to become a brilliant leader of people. Necessarily we'll be looking at some management actions along the way but it's the extra ingredients that will be our primary focus.

I'd also encourage you to read the whole book as a complete text rather than dipping in and out selectively. I've included various tips and summaries along the way if you prefer to speed read, but you should be aware that becoming a brilliant leader is not about a set of discrete actions – rather it is about applying an integrated set of tools and techniques.

Think about it as similar to baking a cake. You can have all the right ingredients but if you don't mix them together in the right way and at the right time, you won't end up with the perfect cake. It's the same with leadership. There are a range of tools and techniques at your disposal but you have to use them in the right way and at the right time.

> think about it as similar to baking a cake

If you are leading people for the first time, you can apply everything in this book right away. If you have been leading people for a number of years, I challenge you to use this book to fill in the blanks. There are bound to be some things you're doing that are absolutely right and this book will reinforce those actions. However, there might also be some things that you are doing that can be improved, or things you are not doing that you should be doing. I hope this book will highlight those areas for you.

I would also point out that the tools and techniques covered in this book can be applied by both functional and project leaders. I have included a chapter to consider the relationship between these two leadership types and how this impacts on staff members who report to both a functional and project manager.

In this second edition I have also added a new chapter to consider how you can lead people without them being direct reports. Whereas leading people should always be about using respect power, when they are not your direct reports you have no option but to gain their respect as a way to influence and lead them. The book finishes with a look at four of the key areas of strategic leadership.

Also new in this second edition, I have suggested some further reading at the end of certain chapters, in order to help you delve more deeply into the subject area. Each of these suggestions is also included in the Bibliography.

Let us then begin our journey and explore how to become a brilliant leader.

CHAPTER 1

Leadership principles

B ecoming a brilliant leader is much easier than you might imagine. While it's not an exact science, there are some tried and tested methods that will help you get the best out of the people you lead. Most of the chapters that follow provide a set of leadership tools and techniques that can be applied whenever you lead a group of people. However, you will find it much easier to apply these tools and techniques if you have a framework to work from, as it will help you decide what to do and when to do it.

This first chapter focuses on this leadership framework, wrapped up under the collective name of leadership principles. It breaks down into three simple, co-dependent models.

1 *Leadership styles* – What are the styles available to a leader? What are the advantages and disadvantages of each style? When should they be used and when should they be avoided?

2 *The competency based leadership model* – This is a model that provides a context for recruitment, staff development, performance management, teamworking and delegation using team members' abilities as the starting point for selecting appropriate leadership actions.

3 *The competency matrix* – This is a simple tool that enables you to capture and monitor team members' capabilities,

helping you to target your efforts and those of your team in the most effective and efficient way.

Leadership styles

There is no single 'right' style of leadership. Brilliant leaders

the real skill is picking the right style at the right time

know that there are several styles of leadership that are all appropriate at different times and for different people. The real skill is picking the right style at the right time.

There are three basic leadership styles – autocratic, *laissez-faire* and shared leadership.

Autocratic leadership

Autocratic leadership is about being in control, telling staff members what to do and how to do it. When overused it is likely to result in a lack of trust and respect, prevent staff members from thinking creatively and taking risks, and create a climate of fear via critical feedback and a lack of praise. It does not generally make for a motivated environment or a high level of staff loyalty.

Sounds pretty bad, doesn't it? But used sparingly and at the right time, there is a place for autocratic leadership. Examples of when it might be appropriate are in times of crisis, when someone is new to a role or to address persistent underperformance issues.

Laissez-faire leadership

This style of leadership is where the leader takes a back seat. They let their staff make their own decisions and give them freedom to work in a way that they think is best. When overused it can lead to a lack of direction, a lack of urgency and staff frustration at having an indecisive leader.

But *laissez-faire* leadership has its place in the leadership toolbox. It's a style that can be employed when leading experts and to encourage team members to make their own decisions and take risks, as well as being a style that can facilitate creativity.

Shared leadership

The third basic leadership style is where the leadership of the individual is shared between the leader and the staff member. It's a partnership between both parties aimed at delivering optimum performance in a motivated and co-operative environment. It involves open communication, mutual respect and plenty of dialogue.

This is the most common basic style that is employed by brilliant leaders. It involves staff members in their own development and performance while giving the leader power through influence and facilitation. There are times when you need to give your people greater freedom (*laissez-faire*) or become more directive (autocratic) but the use of these styles is likely to be outweighed by the use of a shared leadership style.

Most people come to work wanting to do a good job. A shared leadership style creates an environment where people are able to do a good job by taking a degree of ownership for their own actions under the guidance and influence of the leader.

Which style?

The challenge you face as a leader is knowing which style to apply and when to do so. Think about it as a continuum, as shown in Figure 1.1 overleaf. The core place from which to lead is in the middle (shared leadership) and certain people/ situations lead you to become more autocratic or, indeed, swing towards a more hands-off style (*laissez-faire*).

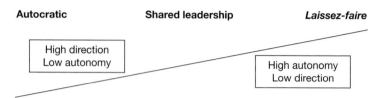

Figure 1.1 The leadership styles continuum

As we progress through the chapters that follow, we'll be looking at examples of which style is most applicable in different situations.

Competency based leadership

A great indicator for which leadership style to apply and which leadership actions are required is to begin by considering what your people are capable of. For example, if you have an expert computer programmer who is capable of creating a fully functioning database in a day, it is reasonable to expect them to do so. However, if you have a less experienced programmer who can produce a database to the same specification but, because they have to refer to manuals and check their actions along the way, it takes them three days, then it is not reasonable to expect them to produce the database in a day. If you push them to deliver within the same timeframe as the expert programmer, you are likely to get a sub-standard outcome along with a demotivated staff member. Against this, if you always give this piece of work to the expert programmer, how will the other one gain the experience required to become an expert?

Just from this example it becomes clear that people's capability drives both performance expectations in the short term and their development needs in the longer term. As we shall see in later chapters, it also drives recruitment, delegation and teamworking.

I have developed a relatively simple model to capture this concept – **the competency based leadership model**, as shown in Figure 1.2 below.

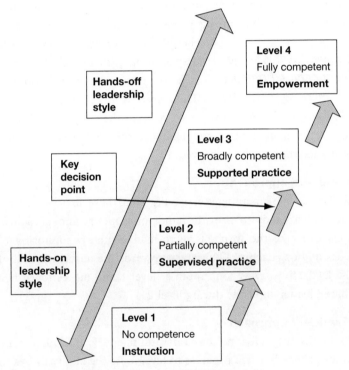

Figure 1.2 The competency based leadership model

Model overview
There are four levels of ability or competence.

Level 1
The first level is when there is no competence in that task area, normally because it is a new task to the individual. At this level the individual needs clear *instruction*. That is, they need to be

told what to do and how to do it and also understand why they are doing it.

Level 2

After getting basic instruction, the individual will progress to the second level and become partially competent. At this stage they know what they are meant to be doing but will have to think

their need at this stage is for *supervised practice*

carefully and critically about what they are doing: there will often be a lack of consistency in their output. Their need at this stage is for *supervised practice*. That is, they need to have their work checked at regular intervals and receive feedback on what they are doing well and what can be improved.

Hands-on approach

When the staff member's capability is at these first two levels, the leader needs to provide hands-on support and guidance. This can take the form of micro-management, monitoring of work and/or coaching. This starts towards the autocratic end of the leadership styles continuum at level 1 and moves towards a shared leadership style during level 2.

Hands-off approach

Assuming the individual has a natural talent or aptitude for the task or skills they will progress to level 3. As the ability moves to level 3 and then level 4 there is a gradual shift along the leadership styles continuum with an increasing level of freedom being provided by the leader.

Level 3

At the third level the individual is regarded as broadly competent, meaning that they can consistently perform the task to the required standard, although they may not be as quick at completing the task compared to the fourth level and they might also struggle with unusual or complex versions of the task. What they need at this stage is *supported practice*. That is, they require the opportunity to practise but knowing that support is available when they need it, along with occasional reviews and feedback discussions.

Level 4

The main difference between level 3 and 4 is practice and experience. Being completely competent at this fourth level means that the individual is able to perform the task to the required standard, within the optimum timeframe. They are also able to deal with complex and unusual versions of the task. To all intents and purposes they can be regarded as an expert in the task and allowed to work independently: that is, *empowered* to get the job done. The leader does not withdraw support entirely but is primarily concerned with monitoring the performance output produced by the staff member.

Applying the model

The model can be applied in two ways – either the person's ability for their whole job or on a task-by-task basis.

Let's go back to our example of an expert programmer who you would generally empower to construct a database to a user's specification. However, if they are required to undertake a task that is new to them, such as making a presentation of their database's capability to management, then empowering them is likely to have a detrimental effect as this would be just like throwing a non-swimmer in at the deep end without any form of buoyancy aid. So while adopting a general leadership style of empowerment for their programming duties, you should ensure they get appropriate instruction in making a presentation (possibly a training course or an explanation from you), followed by supervised practice (maybe get them to make the presentation to you first and/or co-present with them the first couple of times). As they get better at making presentations you would give them

more freedom, perhaps allowing them to make basic presentations independently and more complex or critical presentations
by reviewing with you first and providing them with constructive
feedback. Eventually, they will hopefully become completely competent at making presentations and you can empower them with
this task in just the same way as you do with their technical tasks.

As this example shows, the most powerful application of
the competency based leadership model is on a task-by-task
basis. It's likely that most staff will be a mixture of all four
ability levels at any point in time. Therefore, what they need
from you are different leadership inputs, actions and expectations dependent on their ability to perform the tasks they are
working on.

It is possible to regard staff members as generally level 1, 2, 3
or 4 for their job as a whole and this has some validity to your
general leadership approach to that person – you will spend
much more time with a level 1 person than a level 4 person, for
example. However, there will be times when a level 4 person
has, say, a level 2 capability for a particular task. What they need
from you when they are working on this task is regular review,
feedback and guidance – not to be left to work completely
independently.

Leadership actions from the model

Level 1 – Instruction (autocratic leadership style)
When a staff member is new to a task or skill area, they generally
need to be instructed. They need to know what they are meant
to be doing, why they are doing it and how it is meant to be
done. There are several ways they can acquire this knowledge
and, where appropriate, the new skills required to apply the
knowledge:

● training courses
● on-the-job instruction

- micro-practice with regular checking and feedback
- use of reference materials such as procedure manuals
- eLearning
- watching demonstrations of the task being performed by others.

As the leader you are not necessarily the one that needs to be providing the instruction but it is your responsibility to ensure the staff member is getting the instruction they need. It is also your responsibility to have discussed with them why they are learning a new task and how it relates to their job role or career path.

Level 2 – Supervised practice (autocratic to shared leadership style)

Once a staff member has learned the basics of a new task or skill, they can usually be regarded as being partially competent, but at this point they still need a lot of input from either the leader or a designated coach. For some tasks and skills, staff members may remain at level 2 for a number of months whereas for others they will pass through this level in a matter of days.

Regardless of how long it takes what staff members need is supervised practice. That is, they should be allowed to practise safe in the knowledge that their work is being checked or reviewed on a regular basis and constructive feedback is being provided. Simulated practice situations can also be useful at this stage of development as they provide a safe learning environment – a good example of this would be an experiential training programme such as presentation skills.

The goal you are working towards when a staff member is at this level of ability is *consistency*. This is the main difference between level 2 and level 3 ability. A good example of this would be a learner driver. After a few lessons they will be level 2 for most tasks involved in driving a car, such as hill starts, reversing, parking, steering and so on. They will get most of the tasks right some of the time but it is only when they are consistently performing all these tasks well (i.e. level 3) that they are ready to take their test.

Key decision – Do they have talent?

There is another issue that you need to take on board at this level of ability and one that might involve a key leadership decision. It is during level 2 that you are able to assess (in conjunction with the staff member and any person you have designated to coach them) whether they have sufficient natural talent and aptitude to progress to the next level.

we can't all be good at everything

This is important and often overlooked. The simple truth of life is that we can't all be good at everything and sometimes you will have to acknowledge that you are trying to fit a square peg into a round hole. If the task or skill in question is critical to the person's job function then you will need to either acknowledge that you have made a recruitment mistake and terminate their employment, or alternatively, if they are a diligent employee, look at ways of redeploying them elsewhere in the organisation. If the task or skill is not critical to the job role then you can look at ways of minimising exposure to the task/skill by redefining their job role and moving the task in question into the work stack of another team member.

What you must never do when facing a lack of talent is to ignore the issue and persist with trying to develop them. Not only will this waste your time and potentially cause the staff member to become demoralised but it will also lead to a much greater problem down the line.

↗ brilliant activity

Look for examples in your team or organisation where a lack of talent for a task or skill has been 'swept under the carpet'. What problems has it caused?

Level 3 – Supported practice (shared leadership style)

If an individual has the core talent required for a task or skill, supervised practice combined with constructive feedback interventions will see them progress to being broadly competent. The difference between level 3 and 4 competency levels is essentially practice and experience. At level 3 they need to be given opportunities to practise in a supported environment. Their work can be reviewed less frequently than at level 2, and when they encounter a problem or unusual situation you should challenge them to come to you with a recommended solution rather than just spoon feeding them the answer.

Depending on the task or skill, it is quite feasible that a staff member will stay at level 3 for a lengthy period – often a number of months. Practice, experience and exposure to a range of situations cannot happen overnight.

Level 4 – Empowerment (shared to laissez-faire *leadership style)*

Full competence can be defined as being *capable of performing a task to the required standard, consistently and on time*. Once a staff member has demonstrated that they are fully competent at a particular task or skill, you should empower them to deliver. This does not mean that all support is withdrawn. If they ask for your input you should be happy to provide it, but otherwise you should simply monitor their performance to ensure their delivery matches their capability.

This last point is really important. Staff members should be expected to perform at the level they are capable of. If they are performing at a level or a standard below what you know them to be capable of, you will need to address this as an underperformance issue. We'll look at this in more detail in Chapter 4.

The competency based leadership model provides a simple and powerful framework for many of the leadership principles and techniques we shall look at throughout this book. It will help you understand how to recruit, train, motivate, delegate and organise your people for maximum and consistent results. As such, I shall be referencing this model throughout the chapters that follow.

The competency matrix

There is an extension of the model that I shall also be referencing on a regular basis – the competency matrix – which helps you to consider the needs of the team as a whole rather than just the needs of the individual team members. A simple competency matrix is shown in the following table.

	Team members					
	John	Jane	Paul	Petra	Sue	Dave
Competency						
Presentation skills	1	2	2	3	4	4
Negotiation skills	2	3	2	3	2	4
Spreadsheets	3	3	3	3	2	2
Desk top publishing	4	2	2	1	1	1
Time management	3	4	3	3	4	2
Coaching others	1	2	2	3	3	2

In this example, I have shown a fictional team of six people and notionally six competency areas (most functional teams would have between 20 and 30 competency areas). The numbers in the matrix correspond directly with levels 1–4 drawn from the competency based leadership model.

What information does this simple analysis of team members' competencies provide and how can you use it to improve the team's effectiveness and efficiency?

 **activity**

Before you read on, take some time out to analyse the sample competency matrix. Jot down the key information it provides about our fictional team and how this might translate into practical actions if you were the leader of this team.

Here are my thoughts.

Presentation skills

This team has two fully competent presenters and one who is broadly competent. While the other three team members might need to acquire this skill, it is not an urgent requirement as far as the team is concerned. Sue can also provide support to Petra if she encounters any particularly challenging presenting scenarios.

Negotiation skills

The team has one fully competent negotiator and two who are broadly competent. While this skill might be a personal development requirement for the other three team members, it is not an urgent requirement from the team's perspective. It is a concern that if Jane or Petra need support with any challenging or problematic negotiating scenarios, is Dave a good enough coach (level 2) to provide that support?

Spreadsheets

This team has four people who are broadly competent, which is good. However, who will provide them with support if they encounter any advanced problems? The leader of this team will need to ensure they have access to the support they need from outside the team.

Desk top publishing

This is a major area of concern. Only John is fully competent and no other team members have yet become broadly competent. This means *the team is exposed to a single point of failure.* That is, if John leaves or is absent for any significant amount of time, the team will struggle to process tasks that require desk top publishing skills, effectively or efficiently. Helping Jane and Paul to improve in this area is a top priority for this team. However, it would appear that John has never coached anyone before and so the leader will have to find another way for Jane and Paul to get the supervised practice, guidance and feedback they are likely to need.

Time management

This is generally not an area of concern. The team has five members who are either broadly or fully competent in this area. The one thing to watch out for is that Dave's weakness in this area might cause a problem if he is asked to take on any extra responsibilities such as coaching.

Coaching skills

This is a problem area if this team is to develop and grow. Several team members have skills and expertise that can be passed on to other team members – John is an expert at desk top publishing, Dave and Sue are experts at presenting, Dave is also an expert at negotiating, and Jane and Sue are excellent at time management. But only Petra and Sue are broadly competent as coaches.

Suggested leadership actions

There is not a single 'right' approach to taking this team forward but, at a glance, the competency matrix helps the leader to identify what the priorities are. I would start by getting Petra and Sue to work with the other team members on their coaching skills – even better if there was the opportunity to send these four people on a coaching skills training course and then ask Petra and Sue to support them upon their return.

The next priority is to help Jane and Paul improve their desk top publishing skills. Can John be involved in some form of coaching capacity? Possibly not until he has progressed to level 2 or 3 as a coach. Therefore, it might be necessary to seek support from outside the team.

In the medium term – that is, once the desk top publishing weakness has been solved and the team are becoming more competent at coaching – the leader can look at improving the team's ability at presenting and negotiating. Prior to this Dave could probably do with some help on managing his time better so that he can be utilised as a coach.

> coaching and desk top publishing skills are both important and urgent

The short-term dilemma the leader will face here is how to ensure performance does not suffer while the initial development of coaching and desk top publishing skills occurs. There is not an easy answer to this but it is an issue that must be constantly tackled by team leaders. We will revisit this dilemma in Chapter 5, but for now suffice to say that the coaching and desk top publishing skills are both important and sufficiently urgent that time must be found and sufficient resources allocated to address them in the short term.

⟋ brilliant activity review

How do your thoughts on this team and the issues they face compare to mine? There is not a single approach that is right and other options will be valid as long as they address the needs of the team in both the short and medium term while maintaining performance levels.

A leadership tool

The competency matrix then is a leadership tool that enables you to capture the team's capabilities in a simple, visual form. It highlights where work can be delegated to get the job done and where the team has urgent development requirements. This in turn helps you to prioritise your efforts and resources so that the team grows at optimum efficiency while also delivering results in the short term.

Completing the competency matrix is not a one-off exercise. It should be updated regularly to reflect the team's progress. A shared leadership style would also suggest that it is best to engage team members in helping you to complete and update the matrix. The challenge with such conversations is to ensure team members accept and understand their genuine competence level for each task or skill. Some people will want to 'grade' themselves at a higher level than they really are, whereas others will think themselves to be less capable than is actually the case. You will need to use examples, evidence and good quality questions in order to ensure there is genuine agreement, as the 'buy-in' of staff members is critical to the effectiveness of a shared leadership style.

It is also good to keep a record of the discussions you have with staff members and of each updated competency matrix. The core premise of competency based leadership is that staff members should be expected to perform at the level of their capability. Having a record of capabilities makes it much easier for you to discuss, agree and manage performance expectations, as we shall discover in later chapters.

Summary

There are three core models in our leadership framework that underpin the tools and techniques covered throughout this book.

1   **Basic leadership styles continuum** – This ranges
    from autocratic at one extreme through to *laissez-faire* at
    the other. The middle area of the continuum is a shared
    leadership style that involves a two-way relationship
    between the leader and staff member in order to create an
    environment of optimum performance. Shared leadership is
    the style of choice of brilliant leaders who also understand
    that there are times to shift their style up and down the
    continuum as and when required by the situation and the
    needs of their people.

2   **The competency based leadership model** – There
    are four levels of capability and the basic premise is that
    people should be expected to perform at the level of their
    capability. Improving future performance requires that,
    first, capability should be developed. Each level requires
    a different leadership input and the model is best used to
    differentiate these inputs and expectations on a task-by-task
    basis.

3   **The competency matrix** – This is a simple visual tool
    that captures the team's capabilities. The leader is able to
    prioritise their efforts and resources based on the team's
    current abilities and development needs.

Having laid our foundation, let us now explore the range of leadership activities that will enable you to build, develop and lead
high-performing teams.

CHAPTER 2

Recruiting the best

One of the key factors in leading a high-performing team is to recruit the right people. There will be times of course when you inherit a team but, nonetheless, when the opportunity arises to recruit new people into your team, getting the right people on board will help you deliver the results you require. Recruiting the right people is a key leadership activity.

Most recruitment activity these days is competency based: that is, recruiting people based on their experience and ability. This approach is not wrong and it will enable you to recruit good people but is this enough? If you truly want to lead high-performing teams your aim should be to recruit great people into your team. Let me provide you with a common example to illustrate the point.

When you talk to a call centre what does good service sound like? For most people it would be a friendly welcome, listening to your enquiry and providing an appropriate and helpful response. All of these basic skills can be taught and a large number of people can be competent at handling call centre enquiries.

Now, compare this to getting great service from a call centre: what does that sound like?

It is likely to include someone who actively builds rapport with you, demonstrates that they have really listened to your enquiry by empathising and going the extra mile in their response, to ensure that you have not only been 'dealt with' but that you are completely satisfied. They actually sound happy to have helped you rather than just making you feel like a routine call.

some of these traits and abilities can be learned over time

Some of these traits and abilities can be learned over time but in the main, they are in-built. The difference between recruiting good people and great people is about hiring people with the right personality, character traits and disposition relevant to the role you want them to fulfil.

In this chapter we'll start by looking at traditional competency based recruitment. We will then explore how to recruit for those extra qualities towards the end of the chapter.

Assuming that you work in an organisation that has a human resources department, it is important to engage them at the beginning of the recruitment process. In particular, they will ensure that you are working within the scope of the relevant employment law in your territory. This said, most of the methods suggested in this chapter would be regarded as best practice in most recruitment environments.

Stage 1 – Job description

Actually, you shouldn't wait until you have a vacancy before producing a job description. It is a useful tool to help manage the expectations of staff on an ongoing basis and, given that job roles change and evolve, the best person to keep a job description up to date is the incumbent job holder (in conjunction with the line manager and/or human resources department).

A job description is a useful document for supplying to prospective candidates to make them aware of the role they are applying for and will typically tend to have the following components:

- job title
- grade
- span of control (upward and downward)
- job overview
- main responsibilities
- key tasks.

brilliant tip

Review team members' job descriptions as part of the appraisal process. This helps to manage staff expectations as well as ensuring a job description is always available when a recruitment need arises.

Stage 2 – Person specification

A person specification is a document that describes the abilities and qualities that are required to do the job you are recruiting for. It is the most important part of the recruitment process because it drives everything else. It dictates where you source candidates from, how you screen applications, what questions you ask at interview, what tests you use and, most importantly, it is the basis for your final recruitment decision.

In writing a top quality person specification you are able to influence the recruitment process at every stage to ensure the best person (as per your requirements) is appointed. Typically, the following sections should be included:

- education and qualifications (minimums only are normally required)
- core knowledge and skills (what applicants need to have acquired)
- specific competencies (what applicants need to be able to do)
- personality, character traits and disposition

- miscellaneous requirements (e.g. work away from home, current driving licence, etc.).

In each of these sections there should be a list of the requirements to fulfil the job role. Each item should be labelled as either **essential** or **preferred**. As a guide, the ratio between essential and preferred items should be approximately one third to two thirds, respectively, and this is why *at any point in the recruitment process, an individual who does not meet an essential criterion should be immediately screened out.* If you have too many essential criteria you run the risk of screening out good candidates based on a 'technicality'. It might also be difficult to find any candidates at all.

Let's use our call centre example from earlier and assume you are recruiting for an experienced person. You might state that you are looking for someone with great communication skills, experience of the insurance industry, excellent customer focus and good organisational skills. You specify all these criteria as essential. What if a candidate comes along who excels at three of these but lacks experience of the insurance industry? They might not even get past the screening process and yet industry knowledge might be something that you could impart pretty quickly.

brilliant tip

Brilliant leaders are not in the habit of recruiting 'the best of a bad bunch'. If there are no candidates meeting all of your essential criteria – keep looking. However, this does require that you get your person specification right in the first place, so spend time and effort making sure it is.

Education and qualifications

This is self-explanatory but care should be taken not to include criteria here for the sake of it. What is absolutely required for the role and what would be useful?

Core knowledge and skills

Many of these criteria can be drawn from information in the competency matrix (as discussed in Chapter 1), albeit the focus is on core knowledge and skills acquisition rather than application. An example would be good presentation skills.

Specific competencies

Again, this can be drawn from the competency matrix but the focus here should be on application of knowledge and skills: that is, specifically what they need to be able to do. An example would be successfully presenting persuasively to sceptical audiences.

Personality, character traits and disposition

These are the special qualities that will help you differentiate between good people and great people. We will explore this area in more depth later.

Miscellaneous requirements

This is an important section if there are unusual aspects of the job that need to be fulfilled. Being able to drive, work away from home at short notice or walking safely around a building site are all possible examples. While care should be taken not to discriminate (particularly on the grounds of disability or marital/family status), it is reasonable to lay down key requirements of the role that must be fulfilled by the successful candidate. I would strongly recommend consultation with your human resources department if you are unsure what is appropriate in this section.

brilliant tip

A really good idea when putting together your person specification is to identify the likely assessment method for the various criteria. The options will normally include CV/application form, telephone interview, face-to-face interview, skills/aptitude testing and psychometric testing.

Stage 3 - Sourcing candidates

This is a critical stage of the recruitment process and it is one that is often overlooked or simply delegated to the human resources department without much thought. The best candidates are not always looking for a new job and so a proactive or creative approach will often yield the best results. The main sources of attracting candidates are as follows.

> the best candidates are not always looking for a new job

Internal

In many organisations it is regarded as best practice to source potential candidates internally. This can be before any external sourcing occurs or in parallel with external sourcing. An additional and important consideration here is encouraging existing employees to recommend potential recruits and providing them with an incentive for doing so. Diligent employees will normally try to refer only good quality candidates.

Advertising

This is probably the most common source of attracting job applicants. Care should be taken to advertise in the right medium for the type of candidate and expertise being sought. Options include local press, national press, trade press and, more recently, online recruitment sites.

Recruitment agencies

On the surface recruitment agencies are a much more expensive option than direct advertising. However, used in the right way they provide some important benefits over and above direct advertising. Firstly, they might be able to source candidates that will not be actively reading the advertising media above. This is particularly true of candidates who are successful in their current role but have registered with an agency to be kept informed of interesting opportunities. In particular, recruitment agencies with a specialist focus are likely to fall into this category. Secondly, good quality agencies can be retained to work on specific assignments, often saving the employer significant time during the screening process. This is of particular benefit for small and medium sized organisations that do not have a specialist human resources function or where the department is small. Recruitment agencies can also be very useful when trying to make short-term contract or interim appointments.

If you use a recruitment agency, you should manage them assertively and proactively. Provide them with an overview of your person specification and make it clear that any candidate they put forward must meet the key criteria you have specified.

Education establishments

Universities, colleges and even schools can provide a useful opportunity for sourcing candidates where raw material rather than experience is preferred.

Armed forces

This is often an overlooked area but one where you can find some excellent candidates. People tend to leave the armed forces with high skill levels, particularly technical skills. Most ex-service personnel also have an excellent work ethic. And to make life easier many armed forces (certainly this is true in the UK) have redeployment departments, i.e. a free service for helping you find the right candidates.

Website and speculative enquiries

Many potential candidates will approach organisations speculatively. This is a good sign of a proactive individual showing initiative but, all too often, these enquiries go to waste because there is not an effective system in place for processing them. Smart organisations do not miss this opportunity.

Exhibitions and seminars

This can be an incredibly rich source for recruiting people within an industry sector, particularly salespeople and technical specialists. You should consider networking at such events even if you are not recruiting at the time you attend. Building up a bank of contacts might help you when you are recruiting.

Headhunting

In some situations it is appropriate to target a specific individual either directly or via a headhunting specialist. This is mainly more appropriate for executive recruitment but can apply where particular specialists are required.

Now, take a look back over the above potential sources for recruiting candidates and ask yourself whether your current searches are too narrow. In all cases, care should be taken only to provide limited details of the person specification when sourcing candidates in case individuals try to make themselves fit the criteria.

brilliant tip

Be creative when sourcing candidates. Think about where the ideal candidate will currently be working, what publications they are likely to be reading and what is the best medium for accessing them. Recruitment should be targeted at the appropriate audience in much the same way as marketing targets customers.

Stage 4 – Screening candidates

Once you have people applying for your vacancy the next step is to screen those applications. The first level of screening is to remove any candidates who clearly do not meet one or more of the essential criteria based on their CV and/or application form.

At this point you should consider how many applicants are left. If there are six or less, perhaps it is wise to take them all through to interview. If there are more than six, see if you can reduce the list further against the preferred criteria without the risk of screening out one of the best candidates.

Before bringing all of the remaining candidates in for a face-to-face interview it is worth considering whether a second level of screening is appropriate. This is an area where recruitment agencies might be able to offer extra value. You should also consider telephone screening, particularly where good telephone skills are one of the attributes you are looking for.

Stage 5 - Testing candidates

It is normally best for testing to take place between first and second interview for two reasons. Firstly, it is a waste of time and resource testing candidates who do not pass the first interview. Secondly, you might like to explore the test results with the candidate at the second interview. There are several types of test you should consider.

Ability tests

These are probably most appropriate when recruiting inexperienced staff. They are generic in nature and will normally cover basic skills such as numeracy and literacy.

In-tray exercises

These tests are extremely powerful as they test candidates' ability to perform specific aspects of the job. As such, a well-developed test can help to provide an accurate assessment of a candidate's current competence level. Common examples include a translation exercise to test foreign language skills, a database compilation and interrogation exercise to test IT skills and a workload prioritisation exercise to test organisational skills. More traditionally, you might be familiar with the old copy typing exercises to test typing speed and accuracy and, increasingly, presentations are being used in the recruitment process to test, among other things, communication skills.

brilliant tip

A well-designed in-tray exercise is one of the best and most reliable methods of testing existing competence. Spend time creating your own or, better still, why not get your existing team members involved in creating one?

Psychometric tests

These are frequently (and wrongly) referred to as *personality tests*. Psychometric tests do not just test personality, they also test preferences and character traits. This area is a key dimension of recruiting the right person. However, most psychometric tests used in the recruitment process are potentially flawed in

> the best way to use a psychometric test is in conjunction with the interview

that they are solely based on self-completion questionnaires. This fact does not make them invalid. Indeed, they are extremely useful tools so long as you do not rely on them in isolation. The best way to use a psychometric test is in conjunction with the interview so that you can verify what the test is indicating during the interview.

Stage 6 – Interview

Such is the importance of communication skills to brilliant leadership, I have included a whole chapter on the subject in this book (Chapter 7). The key technique that should be applied in recruitment interviewing is the **communication**

funnel. It is important that you put the candidate at ease and start out with some general, top-level questioning before looking to drill down further. The objective of recruitment interviewing is to discover the truth (or as close to the truth as you can get) about the candidate and then compare the truth to your person specification.

There has been an increasing trend in the UK, driven I think by EU employment legislation, to focus predominantly on competency based interviewing. As such, every candidate is asked an almost identical set of questions, normally beginning with 'Give me an example of a time when you . . .' Competency based questions should certainly be part of the interviewing mix but additionally you should look at using factual questions about the candidate's career and hypothetical scenario questions. The use of active listening combined with good quality probing and summary questions then complete the mix.

Competency based questions

You should use these to explore existing ability based on the candidate's previous experience. There are two problems with this type of question. Firstly, a candidate can make up or exaggerate their answers and perhaps, more importantly, they might not be able to think of a relevant example on the spur of the moment, even though a good one exists.

Factual questions

Examples of factual questions include 'Why did you leave this job?', 'Will you be able to travel abroad at short notice?' and 'What motivates/demotivates you?' As with any question you are not guaranteed a factual/truthful answer. Nonetheless, they are a useful part of the interview mix as they provide specific information about the person who might end up in your team.

Hypothetical situation questions

These questions start by presenting the candidate with a hypothetical situation and then challenge them to suggest which course of action they would take and why. Their responses to these questions will give you an insight into their knowledge, application, awareness, mindset and values. They tell you a lot about the person and their potential.

Probing questions

While competency, factual and hypothetical questions provide you with good ways of starting a communication funnel, the key to getting at the truth lies in the quality of the probing questions that follow. These cannot be pre-planned. They are questions that take the answer you have been given and dig deeper until you are satisfied that you have gone as far as you can. The end of a funnel should mean that you can place a tick or a cross (i.e. a definite yes or no) against one or more of the criteria on your person specification. An unsatisfactory conclusion is when you are left with question marks (i.e. a not sure). This means that at some point, either later in this interview, via a test or in the second interview, you need to explore this area further to discover the truth.

Summary questions

These should be used throughout the interview. Their primary use is to check your understanding. However, they are also good for stopping the candidate from going off at a tangent and, possibly, to highlight an inconsistency or problem with the answer they have given.

Leading questions

These are questions that include the answer you are looking for within them. For example, 'The important thing with negotiating is only ever to give a concession away if you really have to, wouldn't you agree?' I would generally say that leading questions should be avoided because they invariably tell you very little about the person or their ability to do the job. The exception is perhaps if you are recruiting an expert and you really want to test their expertise by 'leading' them down the wrong path to see if they challenge your assertions. However, even in this instance, leading questions should be used sparingly.

 **brilliant** tip

Look for consistency of answers in an interview. Are there any contradictions? If so, explore these further to get to the truth.

Employment legislation

In many areas some managers fear they will inadvertently breach employment legislation by asking an inappropriate question. The approach I have suggested above will generally avoid any problems in this area as well as giving you the best chance of getting to the truth. Additionally, you should avoid asking questions about the candidates' family situation, marital status, family planning, sexual orientation and religion. If there are particular requirements in the person specification that might seem relevant to these areas, it is best to approach them in a factual way. For example, instead of 'I see you have young children, how will this affect your ability to work away from home, at short notice?', a more appropriate question would be 'This job requires that you are able to work away from home at short notice, are there any foreseeable reasons why you might not be able to do this?'

A two-way process

Before leaving this section behind, one further matter requires our attention. The interview is a two-way process. The candidate will also be consciously or subconsciously making a judgement as to whether they would accept this job if it were offered. In some respects the recruiting manager is selling the job and it is best to do so openly and honestly. It can be a complete disaster if staff join and then find the job not to be as they imagined. The job should be presented via the job description and perhaps an additional explanation at the interview, incorporating your expectations, vision and some information on the company.

> the candidate should be encouraged to ask questions about the job

The candidate should be encouraged to ask questions about the job and these should be answered with integrity. While you will not want to find the right person and have them turn the job offer down, it is almost certainly worse to recruit a good person and find that they leave soon after. There is a fine balance to be struck here.

brilliant dos and don'ts

Do

- ✔ Review job descriptions regularly image
- ✔ Produce a top quality person specification
- ✔ Be creative in sourcing candidates
- ✔ Plan your interview carefully
- ✔ Get a second opinion to ensure objectivity

Don't

- ✘ Recruit in your own mirror
- ✘ Recruit people because you like them
- ✘ Specify prohibitive essential criteria
- ✘ Recruit the best of a bad bunch
- ✘ Rely solely on an interview

Personality, character traits and disposition

At the beginning of this chapter I said that personality, character traits and disposition were the difference between recruiting

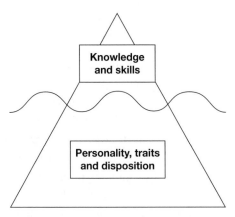

Figure 2.1 Personality, character traits and disposition

good people and great people. Competency based recruitment is all very well but if you aspire to build and develop high-performing teams, a little extra is required. This is best represented by an iceberg, as shown in Figure 2.1 above.

The majority of an iceberg is below the water surface. Knowledge and skills can be trained and coached. They can also be demonstrated and tested through competence and, via this method, good people can be recruited and developed. However, below the surface lie people's personality, character traits and disposition. These cannot generally be trained or coached and the only way you can get the right mix of these in your team is to recruit for them.

Identifying the key factors

Your challenge is to work out what factors are right for your team. For example, in salespeople I would say that the overriding special ingredient is drive. Salespeople are constantly facing challenge and rejection. They are also frequently working alone. A candidate might be a great communicator, dress smartly and have a sunny disposition (all admirable qualities). But if they haven't got a high drive, they are unlikely to be a top performer – sure, they might be a competent performer but high-performing teams require top performers.

it is likely that you
will be looking for
more than one 'special
ingredient'

Of course, it is likely that you will be looking for more than one 'special ingredient'. How should you identify the personality, traits and disposition factors that are right for your team and the role you are recruiting for? You might have an intuitive understanding based on your own experience. Alternatively, you could look at your current top performer(s) to identify the key ingredient(s) that other merely competent performers do not possess. If you do not have any top performers in your team, perhaps an analysis of what is missing will lead to the identification of the factors you should be recruiting for.

Testing for the key factors

The final recruitment challenge then is how to identify whether a candidate possesses the personality, traits and disposition you are looking for. While it might be possible to use in-tray exercises or even ability tests, the most likely tool that will assist you is *the use of psychometric tests in conjunction with interview*. In its very simplest form, this might entail showing the candidate their test results and asking them to comment on certain positive and negative elements highlighted, perhaps asking them if they agree and to provide examples from their working life.

There are more sophisticated approaches that can be used. This is not the place for me to provide an exhaustive list, but in my recruitment workshops I am able to provide people with specific guidance around their own strengths and weaknesses and how to identify whether they exist in any given candidate – a little creativity is required. Essentially though, it is a matter of exploring whether the psychometric test is accurate through carefully structured interview questions.

brilliant example

Let's revert back to the example of recruiting a salesperson with a high drive. You can test for their level of drive by putting barriers in their way. You might offer during the early stages of the second interview, 'I was in two minds whether to ask you back for this interview because I wasn't sure you had what I was looking for.' Now I know this is somewhat confrontational but bear with me. Their response here is key – you are looking for a reaction. The ideal response would be along the lines of 'What were you looking for?' or 'In which area did you have reservations?' They are fighting back but they are doing so in a controlled manner. You can then answer their question by picking on a potential weakness such as a lack of experience or a skill that might be missing. You are looking for a second fightback with the interviewee trying to overcome this perceived weakness.

Now compare this to what the psychometric test is telling you. When the psychometric test results are consistent with what you are discovering in the interview, you can be fairly confident that the test is accurate. Incidentally, this includes an extreme measure of the key ingredient – in our example of high drive, this will often show itself via an aggressive rather than controlled fightback.

When you get inconsistency between interview responses and the psychometric test, it sets alarm bells ringing. Is the test inaccurate or are they faking their behaviour in the interview? You won't often be able to answer that question so employing someone in these circumstances means that you are taking on an increased risk of making a wrong decision.

Such is the importance of recruiting people with the right personality, character traits and disposition that I would question the wisdom of taking too many risks in this area. You see, if someone exaggerates a competency, it probably just means you have to spend a little more time on training and development than you had planned. But if you recruit someone with the wrong personality or character, it will be very difficult to overcome.

Incidentally, the presence of the right personality, character traits and disposition (or not) is often indicative of whether a person will have the natural talent to progress much beyond level 2 of the competency in many of the key areas. That is why this area is so critical. If you get it wrong, you will end up with mediocre performers in your team.

Summary

Recruiting the right people is a key component of building and developing high-performing teams. There are six main stages.

1 **Job description** – A continuously evolving document that highlights the main responsibilities and performance expectations of the job.

2 **Person specification** – A key document that identifies the essential and preferred criteria required to fulfil the job description.

3 **Sourcing candidates** – There are a range of options available and you should choose the right option(s) based on the type of person you are seeking.

4 **Screening candidates** – Candidates should be screened out if they don't meet essential elements of the person specification until there is a manageable number to bring forward to interview (see stage 6). The first level of screening is CV/application form. A second level of screening can come from a telephone interview.

5 **Testing candidates** – There are three options here: ability tests, in-tray exercises and psychometric tests. All have their place in the recruitment process and improve the chances of making a good recruitment decision.

6 **Interviewing candidates** – All candidates should be given the same opportunity to demonstrate their suitability for the role. This entails asking each one the same initial questions, but the probing questions that follow on will vary according to their responses. Second interviews might also incorporate questions that verify the validity of psychometric test results.

The final element of recruiting the right people is to select key ingredients for the role based on personality, character traits and disposition. This is often the difference between recruiting good people and great people. *Brilliant leaders do not settle for second best.*

CHAPTER 3

Coaching and development

T here is a danger that this chapter will become one of clichés, so I will try to restrict it to just the one – *you can bring a horse to water but you cannot make it drink*. This pretty much sums up the theme of this chapter. As a leader you can provide opportunities for your staff to develop but you cannot learn and develop for them.

When we considered competency based leadership in the first chapter, one of the key points was that you can only expect your staff to perform at the level of their capability. It follows then that one of the obvious ways you can improve your team's performance is to improve their capability. It is not enough merely to provide opportunities for your team to develop. You must inspire your team to want to develop and help them with advice, support and guidance along the way.

You must also balance the need for short-term performance with longer-term development, so you will also need to facilitate your team's development with optimum efficiency and effectiveness. As we shall see throughout this chapter, one of the best ways to do this is through coaching.

How do people become competent?

The definition of competence that I offered in the first chapter was 'being able to perform a task to the required standard and within the required timeframe'. Figure 3.1 overleaf shows the building blocks of becoming competent.

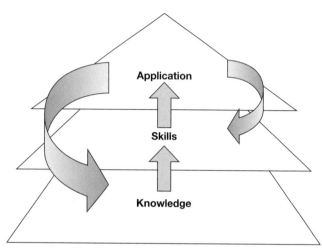

Figure 3.1 The building blocks of competence

Knowledge

The foundation of all learning is knowledge. People first need to learn what they are meant to be doing and how it is meant to be done. Context also helps in this regard, in particular any relationships or interdependencies between this task and other tasks. If people are to learn properly, then in most instances knowledge acquisition is the best starting point.

> people first need to learn what they are meant to be doing

Skills

The second level of development relates to the acquisition of skills. In some instances the individual might already have the required skills (e.g. communication skills) from a different competency area, in which case the challenge is transferring these skills into a different application. In other cases the individual will not have the skills and will need to develop them from scratch.

Application

The final (and crucial) area of becoming competent is the application of knowledge and skills in practical situations and, in most instances, a variety of different scenarios. In turn, the exposure to different scenarios will lead to the acquisition of deeper knowledge and the development of higher-level skills.

▶ brilliant example

Somebody who has never made a presentation before should first receive some instruction on the key components of both preparing and delivering a presentation. This would be likely to include how to structure a presentation, how to compose visual aids, audience awareness, visual–verbal balance, expression and body language. The next step would be to begin developing these skills through practice, ideally in simulated or low-risk situations. Once basic competence has been attained, the individual should be stretched through applied practice in live situations. Through this they will develop additional awareness of audience engagement, how to achieve more challenging objectives, how to handle difficult questions and awkward participants. As their knowledge and skill levels improve through applied practice so their overall competence and confidence will increase.

Tools for developing knowledge, skills and application

The question of how best to achieve these developmental outcomes then comes into play. Consider the following list of possible learning tools:

- training courses
- coaching (on-the-job training by a manager/senior team member/technical expert)
- formal study (e.g. college/university)

- industry or professional seminars
- team briefings
- procedures/technical documentation
- eLearning
- reading books and other external literature
- secondment to special projects
- practice (on-the-job).

When considering our three building blocks of becoming competent, which of these do each of the learning tools help to deliver? In answering this question it is really worth considering each of the tools in more detail.

Training courses

By definition training courses cannot deliver in the area of practical application in a live environment because they occur in an offline environment. However, they can certainly deliver in the other two areas – knowledge acquisition and skills development. Used in the right way, training courses are a vital tool for helping staff development to be efficient and motivational. However, how to get the best out of training courses is sometimes misunderstood so we will revisit this area in more detail later in this chapter.

Coaching

This learning tool should be emblazoned across every leader's forehead. Done well, it delivers all three of our building blocks and, more to the point, it does so in a way where sufficient influence can be applied to ensure the correct learning takes place. We will explore this area in more depth shortly.

Formal study

This learning tool is not without merit but you should remember that it will primarily contribute to knowledge acquisition. This knowledge will not always relate directly to the current job role of the individual. Therefore, you should regard it as a useful tool for the career development of your people but not necessarily a great way of improving capability in their current role.

Industry or professional seminars

Again this tool is not without merit but it is completely related to knowledge acquisition (with the by-product of networking). Depending on the quality of seminar selection, the knowledge is likely to be more closely aligned to the individual's current job than formal study at college or university. You might find this quite a useful part of the mix for developing experts as it will give them access to new knowledge from outside the organisation.

Team briefings

Team briefings are a valid learning tool but they primarily address the passing on of knowledge, either by you or by guest speakers. If you extend this area to consider team away days, it is possible that they can deliver some element of skills development in much the same way as a training course – plus the primary function of an away day, improved teamworking.

Procedures/technical documentation

These, of course, will be almost entirely focused on delivering knowledge to the individual staff member. That is not to say such documentation does not serve a useful purpose but that purpose is primarily knowledge transfer.

eLearning

This is something of a new phenomenon in training and development. Training companies tend to use eLearning as part of a blended learning solution: that is, they use eLearning to address the knowledge acquisition component and the physical training course to focus on skills development. And therein lies the crux of eLearning as a learning tool – its widest use is to pass on, and often test, knowledge.

Reading books and other external literature

As much as I would like to claim otherwise, this book and all others like it can only address the knowledge component of learning. Like professional seminars and training courses, educational books should also provoke ideas and discussion. Nonetheless, these are all part of the knowledge mix.

educational books should also provoke ideas and discussion

Secondment to special projects

This might appear somewhat random to be mentioned as a learning tool but it is among the most powerful available for developing highly talented individuals. I will discuss this further towards the end of this chapter (under the heading of 'Leap experiences'), but in essence individuals with a certain core level of general knowledge within the business and a wide range of transferable skills can be exposed to specific job assignments and special projects in order to learn rapidly. The job assignment element dictates that this also encompasses practical application and so this learning tool has the potential to deliver all three learning components.

Practice

Here we are concerned with unsupervised practice or rather practice that does not take place in a coached environment. As with the issue of specific secondments or job assignments above, unsupervised practice has the potential to deliver all three of our learning components – knowledge, skills and application. However, in isolation, it is unlikely to be the most effective method of development. In particular, learning often takes place in reverse order as the process starts with application (practice) and then skills are developed and knowledge is acquired. Are the right skills developed? Is the right knowledge acquired? More to the point, is this really an efficient method of learning?

What is the best way to develop staff?

This brings us to a key point when considering how best to develop individuals within your team. From the above synopsis of learning tools, it becomes clear that the only way an individual can become completely competent is on the job – applied practice in a variety of live situations. There are several sources of knowledge – books, eLearning, internal documentation, industry seminars, team briefings and formal study. Uniquely among tools external to the team, training courses are able to provide a source of knowledge as well as an environment for developing skills. However, the only place an individual can become completely competent is on the job, ideally in some form of coached environment.

One of the most troubling aspects of staff development that I regularly encounter is this. Managers conduct appraisals with their staff and discuss which areas of personal development are required for the upcoming period. The manager then arranges for the staff member to attend a training course, and once the course has been completed the development area is 'ticked off'. These are not the actions of a brilliant leader.

Is it possible for an individual to attend a training course, return to work, put into practice what they have learned and subsequently become competent? Sure it is, in just the same way that it is *possible* for an individual to read a book, undertake some eLearning programme or read a procedure manual and then practise what they have learned in order to become competent. Any knowledge source combined with practical application can potentially lead to full competency. But is it likely? No, and more to the point, from the manager's perspective, it is completely hit and miss.

brilliant tip

High-performing teams usually have a coaching culture at their heart. It is not just the leader who can learn to coach but also more experienced team members. Invest time and effort in getting these key people up to speed as coaches and you will be well on your way to developing a coaching culture within your team.

Training courses and other knowledge sources can certainly be used as part of the learning and developmental mix. Indeed, they help to make coaching more efficient and often a more enriching experience because people are gaining knowledge not just from their coach but also from other expert sources. But the bottom line is this. The most efficient and effective method of improving competence within a team usually involves a high proportion of coaching because not only does this enable all three key components (knowledge, skills and application) to be addressed but it also helps to ensure the right learning takes place at the right time.

The barriers to coaching

Why then does coaching sometimes not happen as often or as well as it should? There are normally three main reasons: a lack of awareness of the above issues by the leader, a lack of coaching skill or a lack of time. Or, indeed, a combination of these three reasons. Having addressed the first of these reasons in the previous sections, let's look at the second – how to coach effectively. As for the third barrier, we will revisit it in more detail in Chapter 5 when we look at managing workloads and effective delegation.

Figure 3.2 shows the main components of how to coach effectively.

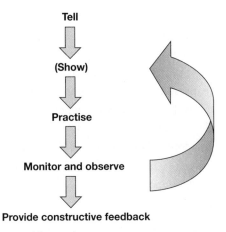

Figure 3.2 The coaching cycle

Overview of the coaching cycle

The coaching cycle starts with telling or explaining to the individual what needs to be done, how it needs to be done and why it needs to be done. This is knowledge transfer and can also be accomplished by utilising the other knowledge sources discussed earlier in this chapter. Showing the individual how it should be done (optional) is particularly relevant to skills (e.g. handling a customer complaint) and is normally handled by the coach or an expert within the team, although some demonstrations are also possible on training courses.

The next stage is for the individual to be provided with an opportunity to practise, ideally lots of opportunity to practise. This practice needs to be monitored and observed by the coach and a judgement needs to be made as to the right time to make an intervention. The intervention requires the use of constructive feedback so that the individual learns from what they are doing right, what needs to be improved and how this needs to be improved.

> this practice needs to be monitored and observed by the coach

As a result of the feedback intervention, the individual might need to be given additional knowledge (tell), provided with further demonstrations (show) or, most commonly, provided with additional opportunities to practise. The cycle then repeats itself until the person reaches a competency level (i.e. somewhere close to level 3 competence) where they can be allowed to practise independently. Once this level has been attained, the coach is able to adopt a supporting role by helping the individual when they encounter problems of unusualness or complexity previously not experienced.

The art of coaching

The principles of how to coach are simple but the difficulty lies in putting these principles into practice. It requires a high level of communication skill and, in terms of character traits, it requires a high degree of patience and personal intuition. Let's explore the skill set and associated behaviours in more detail.

Tell

This requires a clear explanation that is understood by the trainee in question. It also requires (often) that the competency area is broken down into stages for knowledge to be passed on in manageable chunks.

Show

This optional component requires that a clear and 'perfect' demonstration is provided. It is not always so easy to provide such a high quality demonstration in such a way that 'how' it is done is clear to the trainee. It requires breaking the demonstration down into stages, explaining what you are doing and why you are doing it and also working at the right pace as well as answering questions as you progress.

 **example**

Have you ever been shown how to do something on a computer? How clear was it? How easy was it for you to remember what to do when your turn came to have a go? We have probably all experienced a bad example of such a demonstration, which makes the point that a good demonstration requires a high skill level and an awareness of how the demonstration is being received and understood by the trainee.

Practise

Assuming the developmental area is relevant to the trainee's current job role, finding opportunities for them to practise should not be too difficult. The challenge is to find safe opportunities for them to practise when they are new to the competency area, either by way of simulations or the opportunity for output to be checked before going live (i.e. learning in a non-urgent environment). If the competency area being developed relates to a potential career path not related to the trainee's current environment, finding the opportunity for them to practise provides the coach with a further challenge.

Monitor and observe

Monitoring output or work quality is straightforward, as is observing a skill being performed. However, the challenge for the coach is to identify from such monitoring or observation what, specifically, is working well and when something needs to improve, precisely what that is and how it can be accomplished.

 **example**

Consider a presentation skills workshop. These are highly practical events that require delegates to make a series of presentations. When a presentation has not gone well, everybody in the room, including the presenter, usually knows it has not been great. As part of the learning process for the group I will usually invite input regarding what has worked well and what can be improved. While people will often make useful suggestions, where I earn my crust as a coach is to identify one or two key areas that the trainee can work on that will dramatically improve their presentation (other things can follow later). I am pleased to report that I usually succeed but only rarely are these key factors identified by the group or the individual presenter.

The dissection of a skill in this way represents the intuitive component of coaching. Along with patience, this is the underlying talent that is usually required for a coach to be able to progress to level 4 competence – that is, to become an expert coach.

Provide constructive feedback

This area is predominantly based around the coach's communication and interpersonal skills. In fact, the very phrase 'provide constructive feedback' is wrong. It should be phrased 'facilitate a feedback discussion'. A constructive feedback discussion is very much a two-way event as the individual should be encouraged to take ownership of their own development. Through discussion, positives should be highlighted, areas for improvement identified and an action plan agreed. It is also important for the coach to empathise with the trainee so that they do not feel threatened or become defensive.

> a constructive feedback discussion is very much a two-way event

brilliant tip

If a feedback discussion is going to be significant, perhaps covering a substantial piece of work, you should try using the **AIDA** model to give your discussion structure.

● Actions – what did you do?
● Impact – what happened as a result of those actions?
● Desired outcome – how does that compare to what was supposed to happen?
● Actions – what do you need to do differently?

Apart from helping to give some structure to a feedback discussion, it encourages most of the information to come from the person being coached. Your role as the coach is to facilitate the discussion and fill in the gaps when the trainee is not able to come up with their own answers or solutions.

Learning styles

Another challenge in becoming an effective coach is to adapt your coaching style so that it is consistent with the other person's learning style. There are many different ways of looking at learning styles but probably the best to use in workplace coaching is the model developed by Peter Honey and Alan Mumford (which itself was inspired by the work of David Kolb). In the Honey and Mumford model there are four learning styles.

1 Activists

A preference for 'hands-on' learning by doing. Activists tend to have a high energy and low attention span so it is best to provide them with information in bite size chunks. They will be itching to get on and have a go. While trying to accommodate this learning style, you also need to make sure they don't run before they can walk. Because of this, it's particularly important to check the output of activist learners at the early stages of their development.

2 Reflectors

Reflective learners are almost the opposite of activist learners. They like to have time to absorb information and reflect on it before taking action. And after they have taken action, their preference is to think carefully about what they have done before drawing conclusions. Unlike activists, reflectors tend to produce very accurate work which is often right first time around.

3 Theorists

Those with a preference for a theorist learning style tend to be very objective, non-emotional learners. They are interested in collecting the facts, organising those facts into a logical sequence and then applying this knowledge in a methodical manner. Context is very important to a theorist learner. If they don't know why they are doing something and where it fits in with other tasks, they will become very frustrated.

4 Pragmatists

The pragmatist learning style is primarily based around practical application. They will tend to discard irrelevant or background information and only retain that which they can apply. Abstract learning does not appeal to pragmatists, who are primarily focused on what to do and how to do it. The pragmatist learning style is often best satisfied when faced with problem solving or innovation.

Application of learning styles

The biggest obstacle for you to overcome when coaching others is to try to coach in a way that fits their learning style rather than your own. It is the flexibility that is the key here and being able to coach the same thing in a variety of different ways is a challenge. One of the best ways to develop this variety is to engage your staff in dialogue about their preferred learning styles and encourage them to let you know what works for them and what doesn't. The other option is to look at their reactions when you are coaching them. When do they appear to be in their element and when do they look uncomfortable?

▶ brilliant example

Let's assume that you have to coach your team in a new process and they all have different learning styles. It is business critical and you have to make sure that they all understand and apply the new process accurately. How can you do this in a way that satisfies their learning needs?

Maybe you would give the reflector(s) the new process to read through overnight and the next day discuss how they are going to apply it, as well as any problems they can foresee, and agree to review the process with them after a few days of working on it.

The activist(s) would require a quick overview and to get them applying the process in stages, checking with them at each stage that they are doing it right and the process is working.

The theorist(s) would want to understand the reasons for the new process and your challenge would be to gain their acceptance that it was organised into logical steps and was a good fit with other processes. You would need to be open to discussion if they felt that the new process was lacking in any of these areas.

You could probably address the needs of the pragmatist(s) by providing an overview of the key parts of the process and challenging them to apply the process to see if it worked well, encouraging them to feed back on any practical problems with implementing the process.

You could also take this a stage further to see if there are any ways the team members could work together with this process to ensure its successful implementation. For example, you could combine the actions above with a collective briefing and debriefing to ensure any potential problems with the process are identified and solved as early as possible.

Leap experiences

Before bringing this chapter to a close I would like to discuss a high-risk, high-reward learning strategy – **the leap experience**. This phrase was first coined by Jason Ollander-Krane and Neil Johnson in an article published in 1993, entitled 'Growing by Leaps and Bounds'. Essentially, a leap experience is when an individual is exposed, via secondment or special project, to a set of competencies which are entirely new. This exposure is without training or coaching intervention – the individual has to work out for themselves how to get the job done.

> when we throw someone in at the deep end, they will either sink or swim

To be blunt, when we throw someone in at the deep end in this fashion, they will either sink or swim. There lies the high-risk element. Leap experiences are best suited to individuals with a strong natural talent for the type of work involved, high levels of self-confidence and a strong will to succeed. The pay-off is this. When an individual succeeds in a leap experience, their progress along the learning curve is dramatic and their post-assignment performance is likely to be at a much higher level than with any other form of learning. The challenge for you upon their return to the normal working environment is to maintain motivation and continue to stretch the individual in terms of goals and task complexity.

brilliant example

A really good example of a leap experience is when an individual sets up their own business. They might come from a sales background, a technical background or whatever, but when they set up their own business they very quickly have to become good at selling, marketing, buying, negotiating, financial management, administration, etc. As we all know many small businesses fail and often this is because the individual was unable to handle the leap experience. When these small businesses succeed and then grow into larger businesses it is usually because the individual has handled the leap experience well and progressed rapidly in terms of their overall competence and capability.

The entrepreneurial example is merely for illustration purposes, but it makes the point that a well-planned leap experience will take the individual into areas that are way outside their comfort zone at outset. The net result for these high-talent, high-potential individuals if they succeed is indeed on a par with the rapidity of learning experienced by the successful entrepreneur.

It is the power of the leap experience that has led in recent years to me developing a series of experiential workshops. These are programmes that provide leap experiences within the safety of a workshop environment. They consist of a range of simulations and activities that recreate the type of situations encountered in the workplace, stretching and challenging individuals to perform in areas that are outside their existing competence levels. The results have been outstanding. In a short space of time individuals actually develop new competencies (i.e. knowledge, skills and application). The application element is not quite the same as a live working environment but, nonetheless, if there is talent there, the workshops are likely to uncover and develop it. A simulated leap experience provides many of the benefits of a live leap experience but without the risks. There is also a significantly increased likelihood that the learning will be readily transferred and applied when delegates return to work.

Record keeping

Leap experiences aside, it is reasonable to expect staff to perform at the level of their competence. If they are capable of, say, negotiating at level 4 competence but only performing at a standard comparable to level 2 competence, this should not be regarded as a development issue. It is likely to be a performance management and/or motivation issue (as we shall see in the next chapter). Therefore, in closing this chapter, I would like to highlight the importance of you keeping good records of the development activities and progress that have occurred within your team. It could prove most useful if there is later an under-performance problem.

In particular, you should keep the team's competency matrix up to date, but you should also keep a record of all planned learning activities such as training courses, coaching and specific task assignments.

Summary

Staff development is a key activity required for improving individual and team performance by helping to increase what the team members are capable of. There are three components of learning – knowledge acquisition, skills development and practical application – and there are a range of tools available for helping people to learn. Most of these tools are primarily focused on knowledge acquisition – training courses being the only external tool that also addresses skills development.

Regardless of where and how knowledge is acquired and skills developed, the only way an individual can become completely competent is to practise on the job. The best way to do this is in a coached environment but this requires that the leader and possibly others in the team are competent coaches. The coaching cycle is straightforward but requires a high skill level to apply well. You should also be aware of individual learning styles and try to adapt your coaching style accordingly.

An alternative to coaching is to allow the individual to learn through independent practice. The best way of doing this is through targeted leap experiences for high-talent individuals with high levels of self-confidence. These are high-risk, high-reward learning experiences. An alternative to a pure leap experience is for a simulated leap experience via an experiential workshop.

Finally, given that performance expectations should be driven by what team members are capable of, it is important to keep good records of the learning and development that has taken place. This will assist with managing any underperformance issues that might arise in the future.

Further reading

Eichinger, Robert, Lombardo, Michael and Stiber, Alex (2005) *Broadband Talent Management: Paths to Improvement*, Lominger International

This brief but powerful book offers 16 different types of development plan and will help you to take your thinking on staff development to a whole new level.

Lombardo, Michael and Eichinger, Robert (2004) *FYI For Your Improvement*, Lominger International

An excellent and comprehensive guide to career development for all leaders and managers.

Landsberg, Max (1996) *The Tao of Coaching*, HarperCollins

This is one of those definitive texts that every leader or manager should read. It provides a complete blueprint on how to coach others effectively.

Richardson, Linda (2009) *Sales Coaching*, McGraw-Hill

Although normally this book is aimed at sales managers, it provides an excellent template for leaders of all types to take their staff coaching to a new level.

CHAPTER 4

Driving performance

U ltimately, the judgement as to whether you are a brilliant leader or not will be made against the performance delivered by your team. While developing staff will help with future performance, because they will be more capable, it is current performance that concerns us in this chapter.

Consider this question: Is it your experience that most people who come to work want to do a good job? While there are exceptions, it is certainly my experience that most people want to perform well. Therefore, it is your responsibility as their leader to create an environment in which people can perform well. There are primarily three key components required for an individual and a team to perform.

1 They need to know what is expected of them.

2 They need to be capable of achieving what is expected of them.

3 They need to be motivated.

The first and third chapters of this book addressed point 2 – how to assess and improve an individual's capability. In this chapter we'll start by exploring point 1 – managing against performance expectations – and conclude by discussing the third component – motivating staff.

Managing against performance expectations

Figure 4.1 below provides our model of managing by known expectations.

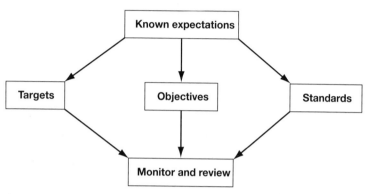

Figure 4.1

As this figure shows, making clear what is expected of the individual can be broken down into three components: targets, objectives and standards.

1 Targets

These are the numerical factors by which an individual's day-to-day tasks and responsibilities can be measured. They should be known in advance, preferably agreed by the individual, consistent with their competence level and directly related to the key responsibilities contained in their job description. Most jobs can and should have numerical targets attached to them, although these targets do not have to cover all of the responsibilities from the job description as long as they capture the main ones.

2 Objectives

We are interested here in performance objectives as opposed to developmental objectives. I believe that one of an individual's objectives should always be to deliver the main tasks and responsibilities as defined in their job description. There should then be additional objectives to accomplish project type outcomes throughout the period in question. These might include contributing to team objectives, standardising work practices, implementing change, developing others and improving processes.

Objectives should also be written in **SMART** form:

- **S**pecific – very clear about what is expected.
- **M**easurable – normally through evidence rather than numerical targets.
- **A**greed – developed in conjunction with the person rather than imposed.
- **R**ealistic – within their capability.
- **T**imed – a clear deadline.

Some organisations will put slightly different interpretations on the terms targets and objectives, including the use of the term 'goals'. Without wishing to debate the issue here, it doesn't really matter what performance metrics are called as long as it is completely clear what is expected of the individual, that they are motivated to achieve these expectations and that it is possible to measure objectively whether the expectations have been met.

3 Standards

It is all very well having performance targets and objectives but the third and crucial component is to have clear standards that must also be achieved, i.e. work quality. Consider a salesperson who has a target to sell 100 widgets this quarter. They might sell 100 widgets by telling lies and making false claims to their customers. Would this be acceptable? Of course not. Therefore, it is essential to have clear standards of work

have clear standards that must also be achieved

quality that must be achieved alongside the other performance metrics.

Standards can normally be articulated in two ways. Firstly, through clear written procedures. Secondly, via the coaching and delegation process. Again though, the required standards must be clear in advance so that team members can strive to achieve them.

brilliant tip

There is a danger that expectations are set and reviewed just once or twice a year whereas the reality is that things change. You should proactively adjust performance expectations as and when required, according to business need. When changing a formal objective or target, be sure to inform the human resources department so that the performance review documentation is updated accordingly.

Monitor and review performance

Once expectations are known, your team members will go forth and try to deliver what is expected of them. It is important for you to monitor what is actually being delivered and to review performance with team members on a regular basis. At these review meetings team members should be able to identify for themselves whether they have delivered their targets and objectives, although from time to time you might have additional information and observations, particularly in relation to standards. Where performance meets the expectation, this should be acknowledged and praised. Where performance falls short of the expectation, the reasons for the shortfall need to be explored, openly and honestly. An action plan should then be put in place to correct or make up the shortfall.

where performance falls short the reasons need to be explored

When your staff exceed the expectation or meet particularly challenging objectives, the praise should be emphatic. You should go out of your way to make sure that their exceptional performance is both recognised and appreciated.

brilliant tip

If your staff have gone the extra mile in effort and performance, you should go the extra mile in recognising it. Praise them in person. Send them a thank you card. Give them a reward. Buy them a small gift.

These gestures will be paid back many times over as they strive to deliver even higher levels of performance.

The other thing you should be thinking about when staff overperform is how you are going to find the right balance between maintaining motivation and stretching future performance. If you suddenly hike up their target by 20 per cent, maybe they will see it as a punishment for performing well and become demotivated. You will need to engage them in a skilful dialogue that focuses on what they expect of their own performance based on how well they have done so far.

brilliant tip

A really good way of getting your staff to overperform without running the risk of demotivating them is to use **stretch targets and objectives**. All this means is that they have their basic targets and objectives - this is what is expected of them. But on top of this you suggest and agree a stretch: that is, give them something higher to aim for in order to deliver exceptional performance. Of course, it also helps if there is some formal recognition and reward attached to achieving stretch targets and objectives.

The performance review process

The formal performance review (often known as appraisal) process is not a form filling exercise to satisfy the human resources department, neither is it a 'school report' and nor should there be any surprises. If you are doing your job well, best practice dictates that you will be reviewing staff performance regularly and doing everything required of the performance review process whether there is a formal appraisal system in place or not. In other words, the performance review process fits in with or supports good leadership practice rather than the other way round.

An annual process is likely to have the characteristics contained in Figure 4.2 below.

Review previous performance   **Plan future performance**

(Review job description)

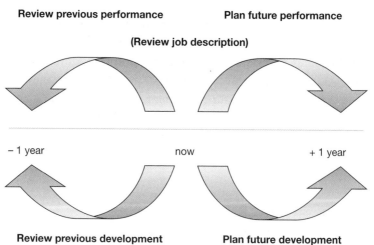

– 1 year   now   + 1 year

Review previous development   **Plan future development**

Figure 4.2 Annual performance review process

Overview

Essentially, there are five stages to a performance review discussion.

1   Reviewing the performance that has taken place against expectations.

2   Planning the future performance expectations.

3   Reviewing the job description (optional component).

4   Reviewing the development that has taken place.

5   Planning future development.

The majority of the inputs to this discussion should come from the staff member. Your role is to guide the discussion by asking the right questions, ensuring objectivity and making additional assertions where necessary. The two areas where you are likely to provide a higher input to the discussion are in planning future performance expectations and planning future development. Nonetheless, the more of it that comes from the individual, the more powerful it is likely to be.

brilliant tip

Encourage your staff to take ownership of the review process. Get them to come along prepared with evidence and examples to support their achievements. Let them drive the discussion as long as it remains on track. The more they take ownership of their own performance, the more likely they are to deliver. It is also an opportunity to ensure their development is on track and for them to express any support requirements they may have.

Frequency of reviews

An annual appraisal process is insufficient for regular performance reviews. Many companies have recognised this and are moving towards half-yearly or quarterly reviews. While this is a good move, you should probably be conducting regular reviews (also known as one-to-ones) even more frequently. This is where it can be useful to refer back to the competency based leadership model and think in terms of the general competence of the person as a whole rather than on a task-by-task basis. The following guidelines show how frequently performance reviews should take place.

- General level 1 competence – weekly review.
- General level 2 competence – monthly review.
- General level 3 competence – monthly review.
- General level 4 competence – quarterly review.

A regular performance review meeting (informal if you like) should have exactly the same components as the formal review meeting (with the exception of the job description review). While these meetings are less formal than the documented appraisal process, you should still keep records of the key outcomes of the meeting. In particular, if there is any underperformance, a record of the action plan should be circulated to the staff member, in writing, after the review meeting.

Dealing with underperformance

underperformance can be successfully addressed by identifying it early on

In most cases underperformance can be successfully addressed by identifying it early on, discussing it with the individual and putting in place an action plan that will get performance back on track.

Continued underperformance is, or at least should be, a valid reason for dismissing or redeploying an individual. Of course, you have to work within the employment laws of the country involved. You are not expected to be an employment law expert and you should engage the human resources department at the earliest opportunity once it becomes apparent that an underperformance issue might go down the disciplinary route.

In general terms, it is unlikely that disciplinary action can commence unless appropriate development and performance improvement opportunities have been presented to the individual. This is not as cumbersome as it sounds. If you have been following best practice in terms of development (as per Chapter 3) and performance (as per this chapter), and keep good written records, then it is likely that the human resources department will be able to progress to the disciplinary stage expeditiously.

If you have an individual who is trying hard but is simply not very well suited to the role they are in (i.e. a square peg in a round hole), the organisation might benefit from redeployment. If the individual is capable but not performing because of a lack of effort, it is normally better all round to go down a disciplinary path that will lead to dismissal if performance does not improve. Redeployment in these instances is likely to be counter productive to the organisation's success.

brilliant tip

Never ignore an underperformance issue. Address such issues objectively and proactively. If you ignore the problem it will have a negative effect on the rest of the team in the short term and give the organisation a problem in the longer term.

If you are following best practice – recruiting the right people, developing them in the relevant competency areas, conducting regular performance reviews around known expectations and, as we shall see, helping to motivate them, delegating effectively, managing workloads appropriately and creating an inspiring teamworking environment – then you are unlikely to encounter continued underperformance very often, if at all.

Informal communication

One of the most powerful things you can do to drive performance is to communicate regularly with your team members. By this, I don't mean micro-managing them. Informal communication is about being in touch with your staff on a day-to-day basis, making sure support is available if they need it, keeping your finger on the pulse with regard to issues of the day and showing that you are part of the team as well as leading it.

Sometimes they will need your input or help in removing a barrier; other times they will need energising or, perhaps, a team member might need to let off steam. Part of becoming a brilliant leader is developing an intuition for what is required to keep your team at optimum performance while ensuring they are also comfortable with your presence.

Motivation

Motivation must always come from within the individual but as the leader you have a major role in influencing motivation. The first thing to be aware of is that everybody is motivated (and demotivated) by a different set of factors – what works for one of your team will not necessarily work for another.

everybody is motivated (and demotivated) by a different set of factors

Although not an exhaustive list, here are the more common factors that affect motivation at work:

- money and the reward package in general
- job satisfaction
- achieving goals
- recognition of performance
- flexibility to innovate
- being empowered at the right developmental level
- training and personal development
- promotion prospects
- influence and power
- working environment

- teamworking
- work–life balance
- relationship with manager
- job security
- change
- stability
- challenge
- competition
- organisational culture
- status.

↗ **brilliant** activity

Work through the list of motivational factors above and identify which ones you can influence as a leader.

Typically, most leaders can influence around 70 per cent of these motivational factors. It is also worth noting that the absence of a particular motivator has the capacity to demotivate.

Your challenge in becoming a brilliant leader is to identify the key factors that motivate (or have the capacity to demotivate) each of your people. Once these have been identified, the next challenge is to try to influence these motivators positively or, as a minimum, to ensure that their absence does not demotivate your team members.

brilliant tip

Have you tried asking your team members what their individual motivators and demotivators are? Why not make a point of asking them at your next one-to-one review meeting?

| people's motivators change as they go through different life stages | People are not always sufficiently self-aware of their own individual motivators so you should not rely totally on what they tell you. You should also be aware that people's motivators change as they go through different life stages. |

The very best motivational leaders will develop an intuitive understanding of what motivates each of their staff. The rest of us mere mortals can consciously pick up on our team's individual motivators through trial and error, observing people's reactions and engaging them in open dialogue.

I hope the above list of motivational factors will point you in the right direction.

Summary

Most people come to work wanting to perform well. There are three key components required for optimum performance: known expectations, capability and motivation.

Performance expectations can be broken down into targets, objectives and standards. These should be clear to each individual and, ideally, they will also agree that they are reasonable. Performance should be reviewed regularly as a dialogue between the leader and staff member. Formal review processes tend to occur only once or twice a year and this is too long an interval for performance to be reviewed. Therefore, there should be more regular (informal) one-to-one reviews.

On-target performance should be praised and over-target performance highlighted and recognised. Underperformance should be addressed as early as possible and an action plan agreed to get performance back on track. Continuous underperformance should result in disciplinary action or redeployment, depending on the reasons for it.

Each person is motivated at work by a different set of factors. It is the leader's responsibility to identify the motivational factors for each of their team and to positively influence these factors whenever possible. Care should also be taken to avoid or minimise factors that have the capacity to demotivate.

CHAPTER 5

Managing workloads and delegating effectively

One of the common barriers encountered by many leaders in the modern working environment is a lack of time to do many of the things that will help them build, develop and lead high-performing teams. There are some key working practices you can adopt that will enable you to apply your time in the most appropriate areas and manage the workload of your team in a way that is both efficient and effective.

The focus of this chapter then is managing your own workload, the workload of your team and how to delegate effectively.

The prioritisation model

The prioritisation model has two dimensions: importance and urgency. The first thing to consider is what makes tasks more or less important and more or less urgent.

Importance factors

- *Consequences* – What is the negative impact of a task not being completed?
- *Benefits* – What is the positive impact of a task being completed?
- *Interdependence* – To what extent are other people or other tasks dependent on this task?
- *Performance metrics* – Is this task directly related to the

performance metrics by which the team or the individual will be measured?

Ultimately, it is a judgement call based on the above factors as to how important each task is in relation to others.

Urgency factors

- *Deadline* – When does it have to be done by?
- *Interdependence* – To what extent are other people or other tasks dependent on this task?

Urgency is primarily driven by the deadline of a task. The interdependency of a task cannot be ignored though. If a single task is preventing other people from getting on with their work or other tasks from being completed, it will often increase the urgency of that task.

Disruptive factors

As you work through this chapter and think about how you will apply the prioritisation model, it is also worth considering some of the disruptive factors. These are real human factors that cannot be ignored but will often disrupt what you are really trying to achieve.

Who?

If a senior manager asks for a task to be completed immediately, people will normally drop what they are doing and do as they have been asked. However, the task may or may not be more important and more urgent than what is currently in that person's work stack. Ideally, the task being delegated by the senior manager should stand or fall on its own merits rather than on the job title of the person doing the delegating. But we don't live in an ideal world and many managers will

ideally, the task being delegated should stand or fall on its own merits delegate inappropriately in this way – it is a fact of life and you must accept that this somewhat autocratic approach to delegation does happen. You should also try to avoid delegating in this way yourself, although in times of crisis it can be unavoidable.

How long?

A task may not be particularly important or urgent but it will take only two minutes to complete. It is perhaps not an unreasonable judgement just to complete it immediately. Conversely, a task might be very important and urgent but it will take so long to complete that several other high-importance, high-urgency tasks will be delayed. In this case, the disruptive task has to be actively managed in combination with other tasks.

Enjoyability

It is human nature maybe to give a higher priority to more enjoyable tasks and a lower priority to less enjoyable tasks. In practical terms, this human failing has to be continuously managed by both the individual and the leader.

Difficulty

In much the same way that the enjoyability of the task is disruptive, so too is the difficulty of the task. Harder tasks are often given a lower priority as people procrastinate over them while easier tasks are often given a higher priority than is appropriate.

It would be naïve to suggest that you can eliminate these disruptive factors as they are both part of human nature and, therefore, part of the working environment. However, you should seek to manage these disruptive factors, minimising their effect wherever possible.

Model overview

Figure 5.1 overleaf shows the prioritisation model. The 'importance' dimension is a judgement call based on the importance

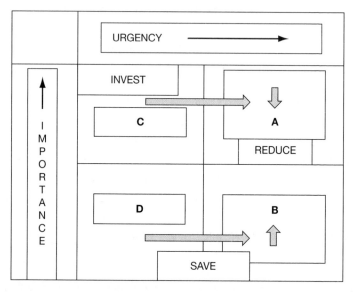

Figure 5.1 The prioritisation model

factors discussed earlier and the 'urgency' dimension is essentially a timeline of when the task has to be completed by – either by a discrete deadline or the deadline created through interdependency. A (theoretical) midpoint is shown on each axis in order to provide language (A, B, C, D) by which we can discuss the treatment of the different types of task. It is important not to regard the negative side of each midpoint as 'low', but rather simply to consider these tasks as either *lower importance* or *lower urgency* than the positive side of each midpoint.

Figure 5.1 also shows the workflows that are constant for virtually every job type (and, incidentally, life in general). Some tasks are already urgent when they arrive in our work stack and others arrive at a lower level of urgency and become more urgent if they are not completed. That is, some tasks arrive as either A or B priority, whereas C priority tasks that are not completed will become A priority and D priority tasks that are not completed will usually become B priority. In normal circumstances, tasks will not become more or less important, they will simply become more urgent.

Actions

These workflows then give rise to three core actions.

1 You should look to **reduce** the amount of time spent on A priority tasks. This is not a smart place to be working as it is high pressure and rushed, leading to lower quality work and a chaotic environment.

2 This is best accomplished by working in advance – that is, **invest** time on tasks when they are a C priority so that as the timeline takes them into the A zone they are already completed or they just need finishing off. *As we shall see, brilliant leaders spend most of their time working in the C zone.*

3 The barrier to investing time on C priority tasks can be a lack of time. Therefore, you need to look to **save** time on the lower importance B and D tasks. Saving time on D tasks is often a discipline issue as they should be done after C tasks anyway. However, they are often the more enjoyable or easy tasks, thus consuming time that can be better spent elsewhere. It is also possible that some of these tasks can be done quickly or delegated.

The real time savings can usually be derived from the treatment of B tasks. They are often reactive tasks and frequently contain an interdependency factor (i.e. other people are asking for these tasks rather than being part of the core job). Possible time saving strategies are as follows.

> real time savings can usually be derived from the treatment of B tasks

Can the task be delegated?

Delegation can be up, down and sideways and is about getting the job done by the right person, including splitting larger tasks into sections with different segments being handled by different people.

Can the deadline be renegotiated?

Most people impose a false deadline when delegating to others in order to give themselves some flexibility in case the deadline is missed. This means that for lower importance tasks there is often an opportunity to renegotiate the deadline.

Can the content be renegotiated or shortened?

This is about doing a job that is good enough rather than perfect. The time for perfectionism is on higher importance tasks. With lower importance tasks the smart thing is to do a job that is simply good enough.

Can the task be automated or standardised?

The more you and your team can automate lower importance tasks or produce standard templates so that they can be completed in less time, the better.

Time allocation

Your first consideration is to look at how you can use the prioritisation model to manage your own time. As a guideline, a well-organised leader should be spending the majority of their time (around 60 per cent) working on C priority tasks. As we shall see, if you are not spending enough time working on C tasks, it will be virtually impossible for your team to manage their time effectively.

▶ brilliant example

If you have been aware of an important task for three weeks but have ignored it and then delegate it to a member of your team with a one-day deadline, what impact will this have on them and their time management?

Certainly, you have just created an A task for them that would have been a C task if you had delegated it earlier. But if they are aware you knew about it for three weeks, they might also resent your last minute delegation and lose some respect for you.

Leadership C tasks

What are the C priority tasks you should be spending much of your time working on? Listed below are the more common leadership C tasks, although it is by no means an exhaustive list:

- coaching and developing staff
- process improvement
- monitoring performance
- providing feedback to staff
- objective and target setting
- workload allocation
- resource management
- planning
- reporting
- proactive communication
- automation
- standardisation
- change management
- root cause problem solving
- business networking.

↗ brilliant activity

An interesting exercise (if you have time!) is to review this list of leadership C tasks and identify, first of all, how many of them you are doing at all and, secondly, how many of them you are consistently doing in the C zone. A further consideration is to think about how many of these tasks will impact on your staff – negatively if they are not done and/or positively if they are done.

Your team and their workload

Having considered how you can use the prioritisation model to manage your own workload, the next development is to consider whether your staff can use exactly the same model to manage their own time. This model can be applied effectively in the vast majority of working environments. The dilemma you face is whether to empower your staff to prioritise their own workload. Of course, you can only empower people to manage their own workload if they are capable of doing so. You should use the stages of the competency based leadership model introduced in Chapter 1 and extended in Chapter 3 to ensure your staff are competent in this area as it is a key requirement for them to be able to work independently.

Effective delegation

The final development of the prioritisation model is to consider its relationship with delegation and how it can be applied, in general terms, to the workload of the team as a whole. To do this, we can make a specific connection between the prioritisation model and the competency model. But first, it is worth highlighting that there are generally two reasons for delegating to team members – *to get the job done* and *to develop the individual*. This can be further broken down as follows.

- **To get the job done**
  - Are they competent?
  - What is the urgency?
  - What is the importance?
  - Is the expectation clear?
  - How and when will performance be reviewed?
- **To develop the individual**
  - Is it relevant?
  - What is their existing competency level?
  - Is the explanation clear?
  - Is support/coaching being provided?
  - How and when will the task be reviewed and feedback provided?

In general terms, if you are delegating to get the job done you will be focusing on delegating to a team member who is already competent – level 3 or 4 competency. This is particularly critical if the task is urgent. If an urgent task is delegated to a person who is not yet competent, there is a high risk that it will not be done well and that there will not be time to check or correct the work before it goes live.

If you are delegating to develop the individual, it will ideally be done when the task is not urgent so that there is time to check the work, provide feedback and improve/correct the work as necessary. Non-urgent tasks thus provide an ideal opportunity for developing the individual (level 1 or 2 competence), but these tasks can also be delegated to people with higher levels of competence, although I would question the value of delegating D tasks to people with level 3 or 4 competence as there is probably more challenging and valuable work they could be doing.

Figure 5.2 overleaf shows the translation of these delegation principles into the prioritisation model. The competency levels shown in brackets represent possibilities but not ideals. I would emphasise though that the correlation between the competency levels and the prioritisation matrix is not always a perfect fit in practice. Nonetheless, it provides a useful guideline for effective allocation of work within the team.

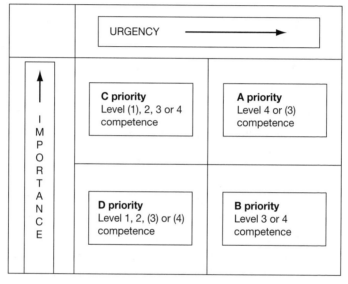

Figure 5.2 Prioritisation and delegation

Summary

Managing your own workload and the workload of your team via effective delegation is a key activity of brilliant leadership as it improves efficiency and effectiveness.

The key principles are contained within the prioritisation model, which is based around a combination of the importance and urgency of tasks. This provides four priority levels from A to D. Brilliant leaders try to avoid spending excessive time in the A zone as this leads to a chaotic and high-pressure environment where work quality may suffer. The majority of your time should be spent in the C zone, which enables a series of highly important, key leadership activities to be completed ahead of them becoming urgent. To find time to work on these activities you will need to find time savings from the lower importance B and D tasks.

The same prioritisation principles can be adopted by your team members, but before empowering them to do this you must ensure they are capable of prioritising effectively. You can also combine the priority and competency models to help delegate to your staff effectively and allocate work within the team. When doing this, you should be aware of whether you are delegating to get the job done or to develop the individual as this will influence what you delegate and to whom.

CHAPTER 6

Developing team synergy

n high-performing teams *two plus two equals five*. That is, the sum of the team as a whole is greater than the individual components. This is team synergy. There is no single, magic ingredient that will enable a team to work synergistically, but there are a number of actions brilliant leaders can take that will help to improve teamworking and maximise their collective performance. This chapter explores those actions.

Cross training

Quite often, cross training is merely used by managers as a tool for ensuring team members can cover each other's workload in times of absence. I wouldn't disagree that this is a necessary use of cross training. When absence cover is the goal, key tasks tend to be cross trained and the most urgent ones covered when a staff member is absent.

However, the time when cross training really comes into its own is when team members are all (or mostly) broadly competent at fulfilling their own roles. By learning how to do each other's jobs they develop an increased understanding and appreciation for what their colleagues bring to the team. Moreover, they are able to challenge the established norms within the team, providing a fresh perspective of how tasks are handled and the processes that are in place. Team members are invigorated by learning new competencies as well as developing an increased sense of ownership.

When your goal of cross training is to take the team to a higher level of performance, it should not be an ad hoc exercise. The cross training activities should be planned, team members should be actively involved in the process and both the individual and team benefits should be made clear.

For cross training to be both effective and efficient it really helps if your team members are good at coaching each other. One of the most valuable investments of your time can be to help your people become competent coaches. This will enable you to empower your team to manage their own cross training plan and own the process.

You will also need to ensure that cross training is taking place at a steady pace. If team members invest too much time in cross training, short-term performance will suffer. Therefore, cross training needs to be fitted in around the existing workload rather than in place of it.

> cross training needs to be fitted in around the existing workload

Knowledge sharing

One of the signs of a high-performing team is that they are proactively sharing knowledge with each other. Conversely, a poor or mediocre performing team often suffers from a lack of knowledge sharing – an environment where team members hang onto key knowledge and information in the misguided view that it gives them some sort of power over other team members. In the case of the latter *lack of knowledge sharing* environment, it can often be seen in teams that are led with an autocratic style. It is often as if team members are trying to score points off each other.

Whereas true cross training requires that a team is reasonably mature in the sense of most team members being broadly competent in their current roles, knowledge sharing can happen from a very early stage of a team's development. I would go as far as saying that it should happen from the moment a team first comes together. Your primary aim is to make knowledge sharing part of the team's culture and, if necessary, to highlight the benefits (e.g. improved efficiency, supporting each other and improved visibility).

The next step is to create an environment in which team members can share knowledge without it costing them an undue amount of time. The main opportunity for sharing knowledge is likely to be team meetings – What are they working on? What are their successes? What are their barriers? etc. – ensuring that only top-level information is provided unless more detail is required. It can also be useful to create a team knowledge bank that all team members can access. This can be via the intranet site or some other internal tool. Sometimes, this can be as simple as ensuring work is well documented and electronic filing is well organised. Project teams or working groups should also have regular review meetings and an end of project 'lessons learned' session that is documented and made available for future reference.

brilliant example

Jill had recently taken over as sales manager of a sales team. Team members worked independently, each covering their own area. Previously, their monthly sales meetings consisted of reporting monthly figures, the dissemination of information from senior management and a group lunch before setting off early to try to beat the weekend traffic. Jill changed the format of these meetings so that monthly figures were shared in advance of the meeting and instead time was spent on practical issues such as sharing ideas for improved sales success, competitive intelligence discussions and constructive discussion around their most common sales barriers. Despite these meetings running much later into the afternoon, team members willingly participated because of the value they got from them.

During the first six months of running these meetings, the performance of Jill's team increased significantly, mainly as a result of her simple yet effective knowledge sharing initiative.

There really should be no excuse for not sharing knowledge within a team. It is relatively simple to implement and encourages the team to work as an integrated unit. An extension of knowledge sharing is for the team to be encouraged to solve problems together and drive change from within the team. This is considered separately in Chapter 9.

Behavioural preference

Apart from the strengths and weaknesses within a team that are created by individuals' progress through the competency levels, there are strengths and weaknesses within a team through their behavioural preference. In Chapter 2 we considered how talent can be identified through personality, character traits and disposition. This is essentially what I mean by behavioural preference. People have natural strengths in some areas and inherent weaknesses in others. While working on improving people's weaknesses will help to some extent, the brilliant leader will look to deploy team members in such a way that their behavioural strengths are maximised and their weaknesses minimised.

> people have natural strengths in some areas and inherent weaknesses in others

There are a number of tools and models available to you in this area, often referred to as psychometric tests or behavioural models. The last time I investigated this area there were in the region of 700 such commercial models and tests on the market. Of the ones I have used and am familiar with, you might like to consider the following.

Tool 1: Belbin's Team Roles

This model covers nine team roles that are potentially required in an effective team. Most people can usually fulfil two or three of the team roles comfortably but would be out of their depth if asked to fulfil roles at the other end of the spectrum. You are likely to gain the greatest benefit from this by allocating roles within project teams or working groups (www.belbin.com).

▶ brilliant example

You are setting up a new project team and when analysing the team's strengths and weaknesses using the Belbin model, you identify that the team does not have anyone who is good at completing and finishing tasks. This means that you will either have to constantly push and chase people to finish tasks off or need to rebalance the team with one or more people who are strong in this area.

Tool 2: Myers-Briggs Type Indicator (MBTI)

This model covers four behavioural scales to provide 16 character types. Each character type has strengths and weaknesses that will directly affect the types of task they are good at and those they are not. This is an ideal tool for helping you lead an in situ team (www.myersbriggs.org).

example

You identify that a team member is an extreme introvert and find this to be consistent with their reluctance to interact with other departments. As they are an analyst this is a minor part of their role. Pushing them towards more interaction is likely to cause them to be anxious and uncomfortable. Alternatively, you could minimise their need to interact with other departments by allocating more of this type of work to team members who are more extrovert. In return, you could move some of their other duties to the analyst to compensate.

Tool 3: The DiSC model

The DiSC (Dominance, Influence, Steadiness and Conscientiousness) model can be excellent as an aid to recruitment. In particular, it is great for helping to identify key personality and character traits that you have outlined in your person specification. An additional use of the DiSC model is that it can help to identify stress (and the causes of stress) in the workplace (www.discprofile.com).

example

You are recruiting a new salesperson and a DiSC analysis identifies they have quite a low drive. You use this indicator to test their reaction to challenge and rejection and find that the test is accurate despite their appearance of being a confident communicator. You decide not to offer them the job and save yourself the problem of having a square peg in a round hole.

Tool 4: Strength Deployment Inventory (SDI)

The power of the SDI tool lies in its simplicity. It is based around just three colours and the combinations of these give

10 core behavioural profiles. It is excellent for helping to handle interpersonal interactions, including perhaps, most importantly, empathising with people who have different preferences. You can also use this tool to help prevent and resolve conflicts among team members as well as helping you to lead an in situ or project team more effectively (www.personalstrengths.com).

▶ brilliant example

You have two team members and you identify that one is an action oriented person who is great in a crisis but who is poor with accuracy and detail. The other is more of a perfectionist who struggles when asked to rush urgent tasks but produces great quality work. These differences also cause tensions between the two team members when they are working on interdependent tasks. While acknowledging that everyone has to work outside their comfort zone from time to time, you are able to reorganise their roles and responsibilities so that one spends more time on urgent tasks that need to be done quickly but not perfectly while the other works on detail oriented tasks that are not so urgent but where accuracy is important.

Some caveats

In recommending the above as useful behavioural models and tools for helping a manager get the best from their people as individuals and as a team, there are some caveats I feel it's important to mention.

- You should be trained in how to use them effectively.
- There is a cost for using the questionnaires and analysis tools.
- There is a danger of 'pigeonholing' people which can be restrictive.
- The models/tools are mainly based on self-analysis questionnaires. This is flawed as people sometimes lack

self-awareness and other times will answer according to how they think they should be rather than how they actually are.

Nonetheless, behavioural tools provide a useful aid to building, developing and leading high-performing teams. Of course, you don't necessarily need to use tools to identify people's behavioural strengths and weaknesses if you are sufficiently emotionally intelligent to 'read people' intuitively. The behavioural tools merely help to support your intuition and fill in the gaps.

Stages of team development

Bruce Tuckman first developed his stages of team development model in 1965 and updated it in conjunction with Mary Ann Jensen in 1977. The principles laid out in this model still hold true today and can be applied to both functional teams and project teams. Figure 6.1 shows the five stages of a team's development.

Forming

This stage is when a team first comes together. Team members are unsure about what is expected of them and what is expected of their colleagues or, indeed, what their colleagues are capable of. People are generally eager to avoid conflict at this stage and so tend to do what is asked of them by the team leader. The team will require clear direction from you at this stage.

Storming

This is often seen as a negative stage of a team's development but it is actually an important stage. As a team starts to work together, tensions arise. Team members jostle for position within the team, particularly in relation to roles and responsibilities.

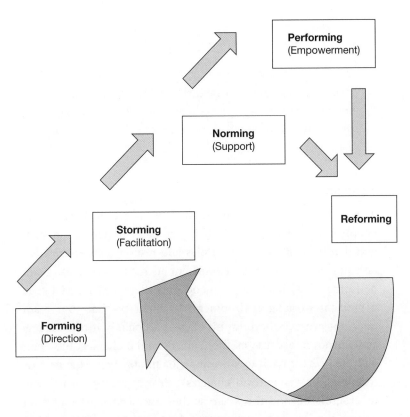

Figure 6.1 Stages of team development
Source: Based on www.infed.org/thinkers/tuckman.htm

There will generally be a lack of trust among team members and certain alliances might be formed, especially if some team members have worked together previously. Your role at this stage is to facilitate the tensions, conflicts and working practices within the team to ensure that team members are both comfortable with their own contribution to the team and respectful of their colleagues' contributions and capabilities.

brilliant tip

Get your team through the storming stage quickly. Set up an away day or similar event and run exercises that take team members through the pain barrier in a safe environment. This helps to break tensions, increase co-operation and bonds the team through shared experiences.

Norming

This is as far as most teams get to. Norms are established and people are comfortable with their own contribution to the team and that of their colleagues. Roles and responsibilities are clear and people are generally competent in their own roles. Team performance is likely to be good and there will normally be a pleasant working environment. It might be that your team does not progress beyond this stage, particularly if there is any staff turnover because as the team dynamic changes the team will then revert back to storming (for minor team changes) or forming (for major team changes). Project teams are unlikely to progress beyond this stage as they are normally focused on getting the job done rather than development (which is a key requirement to take the team to the final stage). Longer-term projects sometimes provide an exception. If your team stays together you have an opportunity to take them to the next level.

Performing

this should be your goal when striving to become a brilliant leader

When a team reaches this level they are producing excellent results and are capable of delivering exceptional outcomes. It is quite a rare situation and yet this should be your goal when striving to become a brilliant leader. Team members are not only competent in their own roles but they have also developed some awareness of each other's roles via cross training and ongoing knowledge sharing, as discussed earlier in this chapter. There is a high level of trust and loyalty among team members. Your challenge when the team gets to this stage is to maintain motivation and high performance levels by stretching them, encouraging them to innovate and continuously improve existing processes.

brilliant tip

Celebrate success. When the team delivers in excess of expectation, make a big deal about it. Reward them with a social event or some other form of recognition that will make them want to deliver exceptional performance again.

Reforming (a.k.a. adjourning)

Great things must always come to an end. For various reasons teams will eventually change. This could be through staff turnover, promotion of high-performing team members (or you) or new members joining the team because of growth. This change of team dynamic will disrupt a high-performing or norming team and as the leader you must recognise this and embrace it. Depending on the scale of disruption the team will need to revert back to either the forming or storming stage before it can move forward again.

brilliant tip

When you have a high-performing team your team members will be in demand. Don't hold them back. It is better to create career opportunities for them in your own organisation rather than losing them altogether. If you are seen as a leader who runs high-performing teams and helps people develop their careers there will be no shortage of people wanting to join your team and no shortage of career opportunities for you!

Team spirit

One of the overriding factors that helps a team to work syner-gistically is team spirit. This is the extent to which people are motivated by their team environment. How much do they trust their colleagues? How strong is their collective identity? To what extent are they prepared to contribute to the team and support their colleagues?

Every high-performing team I have ever been a part of has had this in abundance. If there were a magic ingredient for devel-oping great team spirit I'm sure I could bottle it and become super rich on the proceeds. Leading a team according to the principles suggested in this book will certainly help you with developing a good team spirit but there is something more required. It is about getting the team to think as a team rather than as a collection of individuals: for them to develop a team identity around a collective vision and mission – a team brand if you like. Achieving this is more challenging than stating it, of course, and I would pinpoint the following factors as potential tools that will help you develop an excellent spirit within your team.

Expectations

The leader must provide some expectations for the team in much the same way as individuals need clear expectations to perform (as discussed in Chapter 4). A team vision and mission is fine but it is more important for team members to have a set of ground rules (standards) and some collective goals (objectives and targets) around which they can measure their performance.

Motivation

Individuals within the team need to be motivated. This in itself is not a collective action but demotivated individuals will detract from a good team spirit. If there are tensions between team

members don't bury your head in the sand and hope they will go away – address these issues proactively.

Contribution

You have a responsibility to ensure that each team member is contributing to the team's performance and that any underperformance is addressed swiftly. Carrying unwilling passengers can be most damaging to morale within the team and, worse still, left unattended will cause long-lasting resentment.

Collaboration

Team members have to understand the benefit of collaborating with each other rather than competing. There is no place for one-upmanship in a high-performing team and, in this respect, individual goals and reward systems need to work in favour of collaboration.

Something extra

Team members should be encouraged to do things as a team. This could be anything from socialising as a team to having their own fantasy football mini-league or book club. Most importantly though, this must come from the team members and not the team leader. You can only support the process by perhaps making a budget available or joining in.

Team away days

A well-structured, well-run team away day can be a really powerful medium for accelerating team spirit. A shared experience is one of the most powerful ways to bring a group of people together and regard themselves as being part of a team. Typically, an away day should have a combination of serious business and fun activities.

> an away day should have a combination of serious business and fun activities

Patrick ran a small recruitment company employing 17 people all working out of the same office. The team consisted of a mixture of salespeople, administrators and finance people. Team spirit and motivation were generally good and many team members socialised together on a regular basis. However, the teamworking was not as good as Patrick would have liked, especially a lack of co-operation between each of the discrete functions. As the business was growing rapidly, Patrick identified that this area needed to be addressed so that it did not present a barrier to the company's progress.

Patrick instigated an away day during which he spent the morning discussing the company's progress and plans while also giving all team members the opportunity to express any barriers they were encountering. The afternoon was spent on a fun but structured team building activity that helped team members understand and appreciate each other's strengths and weaknesses. The effect on teamworking and co-operation was so great that Patrick now runs a team away day every quarter. The business currently employs 32 people and Patrick is sure that the teamworking events have helped to integrate new team members and maintain an excellent team spirit.

Summary

Developing team synergy has the effect of a group of people producing a collective output that is greater than their individual parts. It is a key goal if you are to be a brilliant leader. There are several tools and methods that you can utilise to help develop a high level of synergy within your team.

- **Cross training** – Enabling team members to support, help and appreciate each other by learning aspects of each other's jobs.

- **Knowledge sharing** – Proactively encouraging team members to share knowledge and ideas with each other.

- **Behavioural preference** – You should understand your team's behavioural preference in order firstly to know what each member is capable of and then to ensure that roles and tasks are adjusted to maximise strengths and minimise weaknesses.

- **Stages of team development** – There are four main stages of a team's development: forming, storming, norming and performing. Your aim is to take them through each of the first three stages to the point where they are a high-performing team delivering exceptional results. When the team dynamic changes the team will reform and revert to either the forming or storming stage before they can move forward.

- **Team spirit** – The key ingredient required for developing a high-performing team is team spirit. You can facilitate this through a variety of areas such as collective goals, equitable contribution, collaboration, team identity and team events.

Further reading

Gratton, Lynda (2007) *Hot Spots: Why Some Companies Buzz with Energy and Innovation – and Others Don't*, Prentice Hall

In this excellent book, Lynda Gratton examines why some companies buzz with energy and enthusiasm while others do not. Her research reveals four key elements: a co-operative mindset, boundary spanning, igniting purpose and productive capacity. Each of these elements can be applied in the team setting to take team building to a new level.

CHAPTER 7

Communicating like a leader

A leader can have all the knowledge of the preceding six chapters and all the processes in place to implement these principles but there is one key aspect that underpins putting it all into practice – communication skills. In order to become a brilliant leader who can inspire and motivate your team, you need to develop and exhibit excellent communication skills as this is the glue that holds everything else together.

As we work our way through the chapter, I will address the generic skills and then discuss where and how these skills can be applied in relation to the leadership activities we have covered throughout this book.

Core principles

There are three core principles that underpin effective leadership communication. Without these, the skill set we are about to discuss is diluted, often to the point of being ineffective.

Objective(s)

Whenever you communicate with people in a leadership context, you should be clear about what you are trying to achieve. All too often, people focus on the message (i.e. what they want to say) rather than the outcome. This does not allow for information coming back from the other person and nor does it allow for the reaction of the other person. Whether the medium is an email, telephone call, one-to-one meeting, group meeting, presentation or anything else – the starting point should always be to have a clear objective that enables the communication exchange to be suitably focused.

Empathy

This is without a doubt the most important and powerful tool when looking to communicate effectively with others, especially your team. The definition of empathy I prefer to use is *understanding the situation from the other person's point of view, without judgement.* The real power of empathy is not merely understanding the other person's point of view but rather demonstrating that understanding through your words and actions.

> on a human level we all like to be understood

On a human level we all like to be understood and tend to respond positively when we feel that the other person understands us.

Rapport

It is important for a leader to have a good business rapport with their staff. It is not necessary (and some would say not desirable) to be best buddies with your staff but it is important to have a high level of respect based on mutual rapport. Demonstrating empathy is a good starting point for building great rapport but you will also find being fair and reasonable, active listening and showing a genuine interest in your team to be helpful.

The 3 Vs

There are three key tools that we have for transmitting and receiving messages, known collectively as the 3 Vs – visual, vocal and verbal.

1 Visual - high impact

This refers to the part of the message that enters the brain via the eyes and generally accounts for the largest portion of the message that is received and retained. During face-to-face communication the visual message is transmitted through facial expressions, eye contact and body language. Visual aids such as diagrams and pictures also carry a visual message. When communication is via a non-visual medium such as the telephone or email the visual component is often missing. This means that up to 50 per cent of the message is lost.

From a leadership perspective you should ensure that complex, difficult or important messages are communicated to your team via face-to-face communication so that the visual component is present.

2 Vocal - medium impact

It's not what you say but how you say it. This is the tone, pitch, volume and pace of your voice and it has a medium impact in terms of how much of the message is received and retained. When combined with visual communication it can account for up to 90 per cent of the message but when used in isolation – that is, via telephone – the impact reduces significantly.

It is difficult to carry complex messages effectively via this tool, so you should consider using the telephone to carry only relatively simple messages and be aware that lengthy telephone conversations are usually diluted through distractions.

3 Verbal - low impact

These are the actual words that you use to communicate. Clearly, words are important, but when used in isolation they have limited impact and often do not carry the message that you intended. This is one reason why email is prone to misunderstandings. When used in conjunction with the visual and/or vocal component the verbal part of the message is useful as long as it is consistent with the other tools being used.

You should be very careful about using just word mediums, such as email, for carrying complex, difficult or important messages. For example, delegating by email is not usually something to be recommended. However, email is an excellent tool for summarising what has been discussed over the phone or in person.

The 80/20 rule

The 80/20 rule dictates that good communication is about spending the majority (80 per cent) of your time listening and the minority (20 per cent) of your time talking. When communicating with your staff it is very easy to break the 80/20 rule and to talk more than you listen. This is because you will have your own ideas on what needs to be done, how it is to be done and when it needs to be done.

However, as we discussed in the first chapter, a shared leadership style is likely to achieve better results overall than an autocratic style, and this approach requires that you listen to your staff and encourage them to take a degree of ownership for their own performance and development. This does not mean though that you cannot tell staff what to do, make suggestions or offer your own opinions. The 80/20 rule merely requires that you engage your staff in dialogue and, wherever possible, you facilitate a discussion where they reach the right conclusions and answers for themselves.

> the 80/20 rule merely requires that you engage your staff in dialogue

The key here is to listen actively with both your eyes and your ears. 'Listen' to people's body language and facial expressions. If a staff member looks confused, they probably are, so seek to clarify the situation. If a staff member looks like they disagree with you, invite their objection and discuss the issue. If a staff member looks like they have something to say, they probably do, so invite their opinion. When listening with your ears you should listen to what people are actually saying, but also try to assess the underlying meaning behind their message as well as trying to 'listen' to what they are *not* saying. Things that people avoid talking about can often highlight a lack of understanding or appreciation of the issues.

The 80/20 rule can be applied in all one-to-one communications with team members such as coaching, performance reviews and feedback discussions.

brilliant example

Cast your mind back to the last time you had a meaningful conversation with someone at work. While they were speaking, how often were you thinking about what to say next? And while you were thinking about what to say next, how well were you listening?

brilliant tip

Active listening is a challenging skill that requires continuous practice and a high level of concentration. You can practise the 80/20 rule and active listening whenever you are interacting with people either inside or outside of work. Don't wait for a formal situation, start practising this key skill today.

The communication funnel

The communication funnel is an extension of the 80/20 rule and is shown below.

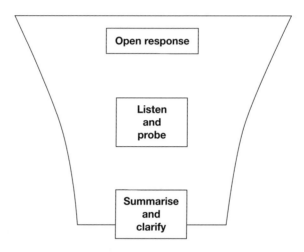

Figure 7.1 The communication funnel

Overview

The communication funnel provides a structured approach to the communication exchange. The end of the funnel is the key information that comes from the discussion and is likely to be directly related to your communication objective – for example, an action plan. In order to get to the end of the funnel, there are two earlier steps. Firstly, you need to obtain an open response from the other person by getting them to talk about the subject. Based on this response you then need to listen actively to what they are saying and probe further with related questions in order to reach the desired outcome at the end of the funnel.

Open response

This may be as simple as asking a single open question in order to get the staff member talking about the subject under discussion, such as *'How have you been getting on with task X?'* However, some staff will not take this as a cue to open up and will provide you with a closed answer, such as *'Fine!'* In these instances your challenge is to get them to open up, and to do this you will need to ask more specific questions, such as, *'What problems have you encountered?'*, *'What were the key challenges?'* or *'Where did you get the key information from?'*

Listen and probe

Once the staff member is speaking openly about the subject, the next step is to shape the conversation by listening actively to what they are saying (as per the 80/20 rule) and to probe further using linked questions – that is, your follow-on questions should be directly related to what they are saying but should move the discussion in the direction you desire.

The problem with taking this technique literally is that probing question after probing question will begin to feel like an interrogation. A key skill here is to be able to probe while making it feel like a conversation. To do this you should offer suggestions, examples and ideas of your own in order to stimulate a response from the other person, often using a question or a pause at the end of a statement in order to get a reaction.

> a key skill here is to be able to probe while making it feel like a conversation

Once you have got all the relevant background information and are getting towards the end of the funnel, the time is ripe to ask more direct questions. These are the type of questions that might have appeared threatening if used too early but now they are a natural progression and the other person is likely to be ready to provide an answer.

 **example**

'What do you think you should do differently next time?' If asked too early in the conversation this question is likely to give rise to a defensive reaction as the staff member perhaps does not yet realise what they have done wrong or why. By exploring the actions and their impact first, the same question asked later in the conversation is likely to have a more constructive result.

Summarise and clarify

Communication funnels come in all different shapes and sizes. Some are complex conversations where a lot of information is exchanged and others can be very simple conversations where you can go from the top to the end of the funnel with just three or four questions.

Summarising key points during a discussion is important to ensure that there is a common understanding and agreement between you and the staff member. Whether the conversation is complex or simple, it is vital that all the main points, particularly actions, are summarised at the end of the discussion.

Multiple funnels

There are some leadership communication exchanges where you will need to use multiple funnels. You should regard a single funnel as being a conversation around a single subject. If you are discussing multiple subjects, you should regard each subject as a different funnel. Mostly, you will work through one funnel at a time before moving onto the next. However, as your skill in using the funnel technique reaches a higher level, you might also like to try moving between the funnels during the conversation when there is a natural opportunity to do so as this enables a more fluent conversation to take place. If you do this, your level of concentration will have to be very high to ensure that you actually conclude each funnel without leaving any loose ends.

The power of funnelling

The communication funnel is the key technique that you should use for having effective communication exchanges with your staff, especially one-to-one discussions. The technique enables you to have structured conversations with your staff so that they reach the right conclusions and outcomes for themselves but under your guidance. This is extremely powerful and there are a wide range of leadership situations where the funnel technique can be employed, including:

- coaching sessions
- feedback sessions
- performance review meetings
- appraisal interviews
- recruitment interviews
- problem solving and action planning discussions.

Beyond conversations with your team members, the funnel is a great technique to use when trying to influence others and/or consult with other parts of the organisation.

---

brilliant example

The following is an example of what a funnel conversation might look like for a feedback discussion, using the AIDA format introduced in Chapter 3.

Leader: Let's talk about progress on the intern programme. What have you done this week?

Staff member: I sent an email to all the senior management team asking each of them to nominate a person to work on the project.

L: What response have you had from the senior management team?

S: Not as good as I was hoping for. Three of them have put forward a departmental manager. Two have put forward previous graduate recruits and the other five haven't responded at all.

L: What were you hoping for?

S: I really wanted all of them to nominate a departmental manager or at least a team leader so that we could develop recruiting profiles that met with management expectations. I also hoped they would be more committed to this project given that it is a senior management initiative but most of them don't seem to be placing such a high priority on it judging by their response.

L: I understand your frustration but you need to understand that they are all really busy people and they have lots of pressing priorities. It seems our challenge is to get this project higher up their agenda. What were the key points you asked for in your email?

S: I have a copy of it here. As you can see I told them all about the project and what we were trying to achieve. I then explained we needed a key person to be nominated from each division and that their time commitment would be around one to two hours per month. I also put in a deadline for the end of the week. I'm not sure what more I could have done.

L: Let's take a look at this the other way round. If you are a busy senior manager with multiple high priorities, how does this email read to you?

S: What do you mean?

L: Well, the first two paragraphs tell them about the project but they were already part of making the decision to launch this project in the first place.

S: So you think maybe I should have got straight to the point?

L: Perhaps just a sentence explaining that you were co-ordinating the project. Then there is the request for them to nominate a key person but you don't state what you mean by key person or what type of input you'll be requiring from them. How could you have made this clearer?

S: I guess I could have been more specific about wanting them to nominate a manager and also provided them with an outline of the project plan.

L: I think that would have been helpful, especially if you could have done this with a series of bullet points. So, what are your thoughts on the best way to take this forward?

S: I guess I should send a follow-up email that is more specific and also outlines the project plan.

L: I think that's a good idea, when can you get it done by?

S: I should be able to get it done by lunchtime.

L: Excellent. I think you should produce two emails. One to the three people who have nominated the right person, simply attaching the project plan for their information. The other should be to the non-respondents, attaching the project plan as a series of bullet points along with a request for them to nominate a manager or team leader to work on the project with an end of week deadline. The other two who have nominated the wrong type of person I think you should call and say what you had in mind and why. Then ask them to nominate a manager. How does that sound?

S: That makes a lot of sense.

L: Would it be helpful if I looked over the emails before you send them?

S: I'd really appreciate that.

L: Great, I'll look over them this afternoon so you can get them sent by the end of the day. We've also got a senior management meeting on Wednesday and I'll remind them all of the urgency during that meeting.

S: Thanks, I'll get on with writing these emails.

The black box effect

The black box effect is something that happens to most people, most days. It is when there is some level of misunderstanding between two people. This can be a complete misunderstanding (quite rare), a partial misunderstanding or a partial under-standing. Whatever the level of misunderstanding or the lack of

> misunderstanding or the lack of understanding can be quite damaging and obstructive

understanding, such instances can be quite damaging and obstructive as far as leadership communication is concerned. For example, what will happen if you delegate a task to a member of your team and they only partially understand what is expected of them?

Figure 7.2 below shows the black box effect and how to manage it effectively.

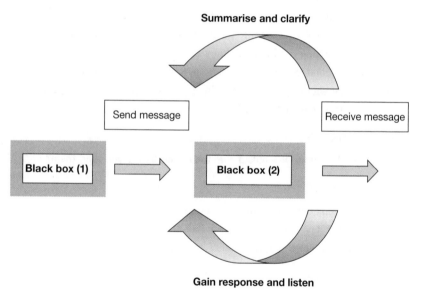

Figure 7.2 The black box effect

Overview

Black box (1) is the sender's brain and their message gets coded (i.e. they decide on the way to express their message) before delivering it to the receiver's brain (Black box (2)) where it gets decoded (i.e. they try to make sense of what is being said).

Managing the black box effect

Whenever two people are communicating, the black box effect is likely to come into play. The key thing is that you get into the habit of managing it. If you are the listener, this is easily accomplished by summarising what the other person is saying. If you are the speaker and the other person is summarising what you are saying, this will normally be sufficient to confirm that they have understood you. However, if they are not summarising you should not fall into the trap of assuming that they have understood you.

The trick is to get them to confirm their understanding by gaining a response to key parts of your message. Questions like *'Do you understand?'* or *'Are you okay with that?'* are not sufficient as they will normally generate a 'yes' response, which only confirms that they think they have understood your message. Better questions are ones that generate a meaningful response, for example:

● What are your thoughts on that?

● What impact do you think that will have?

● What problems do you think we might encounter?

● How do you think we should handle this?

In addition to gaining a response to your key messages you can minimise the chances of a misunderstanding in the first place by following three further communication guidelines.

1 **KISS** – Keep it Short and Simple. By not overcomplicating your message you reduce the chances of it being misunderstood.

2 **Common language** – The thing to watch out for here is the use of jargon and acronyms. It is okay to use them as long as you are sure the other person understands their meaning. Otherwise, you should avoid the use of jargon or acronyms that might lead to misunderstandings.

3 **The 3 Vs** – As discussed earlier in this chapter, visual and vocal parts of the message have a much greater impact than the words on their own. The more complex the message, the more you need to make sure you are using visual and vocal tools to get your message across. Key points can always be confirmed in writing afterwards.

Application

The black box effect can occur whenever people communicate but there are some specific areas of leadership communication where managing the black box effect is paramount. These would include coaching, delegating, performance reviews and action planning. It is not difficult to do but is an area that, if over-looked, can be extremely damaging and obstructive.

Assertiveness

This is a key area if you are looking to build respect based rapport with your team and create an environment of open communication. To begin, we should consider the assertiveness continuum as shown in Figure 7.3 below.

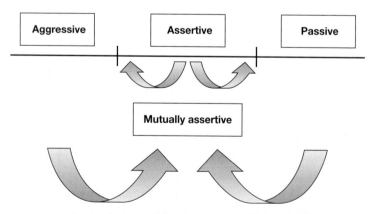

Figure 7.3 The assertiveness continuum

Overview

The best place for two people to communicate is in the middle of the assertiveness continuum: that is, when both people are mutually assertive. This is when both people

> both people are happy having an open exchange of views

are happy having an open exchange of views, sharing ideas, questioning and challenging each other. It is completely consistent with the shared leadership approach introduced in Chapter 1. The problem occurs when one person is more or less assertive than the other. Brilliant leaders are aware of this and are able to adjust their level of assertiveness accordingly.

Dealing with aggressive behaviour

When you are dealing with somebody who is more assertive than you, their behaviour will often be perceived as aggressive. This does not necessarily mean they are shouting and screaming, but it will often mean that their behaviour (whether intended or not) comes across as being dominating or intimidating, often aimed at the person rather than being neutral and objective. In this situation you need to adopt a technique known as **asserting up**: that is, increasing your own level of assertiveness (without becoming aggressive) to the point at which the other person's behaviour modifies into an area that is mutually assertive.

Dealing with passive behaviour

If you are generally an assertive person this is the area where you are likely to need to adapt your style when dealing with people who are less assertive than you. This is especially true if your staff lack confidence, are in awe of you or if you have used position power in the past. In order to have a mutually assertive exchange with somebody who is less assertive than you, the technique you should adopt is known as **asserting down**. This requires that you reduce your level of assertiveness (without becoming non-assertive) in order to draw the other person up into an area where you can communicate on an equal footing.

brilliant example

Jane was an assertive manager. Her style was quite direct but she dealt in facts and treated her staff fairly. John, one of Jane's team, felt intimidated by Jane's direct style and felt unable to challenge her given that she was his boss.

Jane had decided to introduce a new process that she felt would enhance the efficiency of the team. She outlined this process at a team meeting and asked if anyone could foresee any problems with it. John felt that it would cause some quality issues and had some good ideas about how to adjust Jane's proposed process to keep the efficiency improvements but without risking quality. However, he did not feel confident enough to speak up – the last time he had done so Jane had said he was not being supportive.

Jane pushed ahead with the new process and, sure enough, John's concerns about quality came to fruition, which led to the team having to do a lot of fire fighting. Eventually, John plucked up the courage to make his suggestions about how to improve the new process. 'Those are great ideas John,' said Jane, 'but I do wish you had come up with them earlier as it would have saved us all a lot of time and trouble.'

John wasn't sure whether he was being praised for his ideas or told off for not saying something earlier.

Assertiveness tools and techniques

There are a number of tools and techniques for being assertive. Some should be used all the time, whereas others provide an opportunity for you to slide up and down the assertiveness continuum. The ones that should be used all the time are:

- empathy
- active listening
- focusing on facts and issues (not the person)
- good quality questions
- being non-emotional.

The tools and techniques that enable you to slide up and down the scale are:

- body and hand language
- eye contact
- facial expressions
- pace, tone and volume of speech
- directness of language.

Adjusting your style

If you are going to have mutually assertive and open exchanges with your staff, it is imperative that you get into the habit of asserting up and down, depending on the level of assertiveness being exhibited by the person or people you, are dealing with. If you don't do this there are likely to be members of your own team who do not speak up or challenge you, and there will be others, both inside and outside your team, who are able to get their own way by being overly forceful. Neither is a good state of play. Brilliant leaders are able to adjust their style to find an appropriate assertiveness balance for communicating with their own staff and others outside the team. As a result they are able to develop relationships based on mutual respect and open communication.

> brilliant leaders are able to adjust their style

Team meetings and briefings

One of the areas where a brilliant leader can have a massive impact on their staff is via team meetings and briefings. This provides you with an excellent opportunity to motivate and inspire your people. Being able to run an effective team meeting or briefing is a key skill that you should develop. The format and key principles are relatively straightforward but, as with most aspects of effective communication, the skill level required is high.

Clear objective(s)

You should make it clear at the beginning of the meeting (or even beforehand) what you are trying to achieve as a group. Your objective(s) should be clear and specific without being overengineered. For example, developing an action plan to solve a particular issue is a good objective, but to have decided in advance what that action plan will be is likely to be over-engineered as it doesn't take into account any good ideas or inputs the team might have. Clear objective(s) provide the group with focus and are a tool that you can use to keep the meeting on track.

Preparation

Most of the time you should ask your team to do some preparation ahead of a meeting or briefing. As a minimum this should include thinking about the issue(s) under discussion but could also extend to research or presentation tasks.

Agenda

An agenda is a plan of how your meeting is to be structured. It should be regarded as a flexible document: that is, you should only move away from the agenda if it helps you to achieve your objective(s).

Facilitation

Your primary role as leader of the meeting is to guide the group towards achieving the objective(s). You do this by facilitating discussion and making skilled interventions. To start you should state what the problem, issue or opportunity is and then challenge the group to find a way forward by asking questions that encourage relevant inputs from them. Everyone should be encouraged to speak but only if they have something relevant to say. There is a balance to be struck between team members who contribute enthusiastically and when this spills over to become dominating. When a team member begins to dominate you can usually control their contributions by asking others if they have any comment to make. If this does not work, you might need to curtail the dominant contributor by pointing out that they need to give others a chance to contribute.

The other aspect of facilitation is to ensure the meeting keeps progressing. If a contributor starts to go off at a tangent, bring them back on track with a question. Once a point has been made or agreed, move the group onto the next point. If there is a blockage or disagreement, summarise the state of play and pose a question to move the group on.

Actions

Most of the time, team meetings and briefings result in actions (except where the objective is merely to inform). All actions should be summarised, responsibility allocated and a deadline agreed. These should then be confirmed in writing as soon as possible after the meeting.

brilliant tip

Keep it fresh. Try to avoid team meetings and briefings becoming stale by changing the format and encouraging team members to take some ownership of their meetings. Asking people to present success stories, sharing ideas for improvement and recognising outstanding performance are all ways of doing this.

Summary

Communicating effectively is an essential leadership skill as it underpins virtually all leadership activities. The core principles are to have a clear objective for each communication exchange, to develop and demonstrate empathy and to build respect based rapport.

Key communication techniques include the 3 Vs (visual, vocal and verbal), the 80/20 rule and the black box effect. The most critical technique for a brilliant leader is the communication funnel as this enables a structured and controlled conversation to take place. You should also adopt an appropriate level of assertiveness in relation to the people you are communicating with – the goal being mutually assertive communication exchanges.

Finally, team meetings and briefings provide an excellent opportunity for you to inspire and motivate your team. You should ensure these meetings and briefings have clear objectives and a structured agenda. People should be encouraged to prepare in advance and make valid contributions. These contributions need to be facilitated (usually by you) and all actions and agreements summarised at the end of the meeting and confirmed in writing.

Further reading

Patterson, Kerry, Grenny, Joseph, McMillan, Ron and Switzler, Al (2002) *Crucial Conversations: Tools for Talking When Stakes Are High*, McGraw-Hill

This widely acclaimed text provides leaders with an excellent set of tools for handling high-stakes conversations.

CHAPTER 8

Leading cross functional teams

ncreasingly, larger organisations (especially those with a technology focus) are adopting a matrix management approach to provide flexibility and efficient use of resources. This is not as complex as it sounds. Staff members sit in functional teams where all team members share a common expertise. They are then allocated to project teams (sometimes referred to as virtual teams) to work on specific projects or assignments alongside other staff members who are drawn from different functional teams.

Strategically, this approach makes a great deal of sense, but on the ground level it causes leadership challenges for both the functional team leader and the cross functional or project team leader. The challenges faced by both of these leaders directly impact on the staff members within their span of control in terms of performance management, personal development and motivation.

The focus of this chapter is to provide some guidance as to how leaders can successfully face these challenges.

The eternal triangle

Figure 8.1 overleaf shows the three-way relationship that is created when staff operate in cross functional teams.

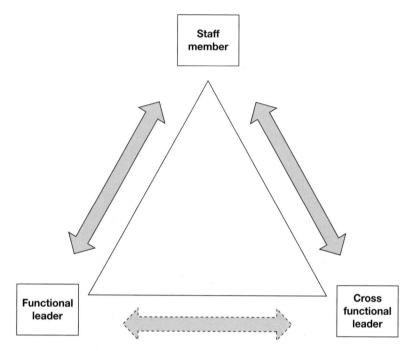

Figure 8.1 The eternal triangle

Functional leadership

The functional leader has a remote relationship with the staff member. They are primarily responsible for maintaining and developing the expertise within the functional team. This is likely to entail knowledge sharing, learning and development activities, coaching and maintaining an up-to-date competency matrix. Additionally, the functional leader is normally responsible for conducting appraisal interviews with their functional team members which, as we saw in Chapter 4, includes a mix between performance and development discussions, both past and projected.

Cross functional leadership

The cross functional leader has a day-to-day relationship with the staff member. They are responsible for putting the team together based mainly on existing capability and then delivering the performance

> the cross functional leader has a day-to-day relationship with the staff member

objectives of their project or assignment. The cross functional leader has little interest or incentive in developing staff as this falls outside their focus of delivering against shorter-term performance metrics.

The staff member

The staff member in the eternal triangle has a relationship with both their functional leader and their cross functional leader(s). They interact with their functional leader for ongoing development issues and periodic appraisal discussions, whereas they interact with their cross functional leader(s) for day-to-day performance issues. An added complication here is that a staff member might have just a single cross functional leader if they are working on a major project or several cross functional leaders if they are working on a series of smaller projects or discrete assignments.

The challenges

It is clear that there are some obvious conflicts and challenges created by cross functional working. The first is that there is often little or no communication between the functional leader and the cross functional leader. The second is that there might be several cross functional leaders involved simultaneously, which creates obvious conflicts on the time allocation of the individual staff member. The third and perhaps most hazardous challenge is the conflict between the role of the functional leader (focus on staff development) and that of the cross functional leader (focus on staff performance).

brilliant example

Michael was a project manager who had a tight delivery schedule for a high-profile technical application. Two of his team informed him that they had been booked on a three-day advanced database design course at the end of the month. This was the first Michael had heard about it and he identified that it would lead to his project being delivered late, affecting both his bonus and his reputation within the business. His response was to tell the two staff members that they couldn't go on the course and would need either to cancel it or to reschedule it for after the project was finished.

The two staff members, Pauline and Ken, were extremely disappointed as they had been trying to get on this course for over six months. They tried to contact their functional manager to resolve the issue but found that he was on leave until the end of the following week. They had no option but to cancel their attendance. When Martin, their functional manager, returned from leave he was livid that they had cancelled the course as the fee would still have to be paid. He informed Pauline and Ken that they would have to wait until the next financial year until he would even consider sending them on the course again, which, in turn, meant that they would both fail to meet a key development objective this year. They both felt that they were being punished for a chain of events that was outside their control.

An added complication in these relationships is that the functional leadership role is not always a full-time one. The functional leader might also be assigned to work on projects, leaving them with limited time to liaise with the cross functional leaders, communicate with their own functional team members and to develop or coach them.

The solutions

There are no easy answers to the challenges presented by cross functional working, but there are some best practice principles and processes that can be employed to make this type of working both efficient and effective.

Roles and responsibilities

If cross functional working is to be effective, the roles and responsibilities of all parties must be clearly defined. More to the point, these definitions need to include expectations that overcome some of the challenges.

Cross functional leaders should have a clear responsibility to report on performance to the functional leader and provide evidence to support this feedback. It is a moot point whether they should also be encouraged to allow time for staff development activities, including exposure to tasks that will stretch individuals and allow them to improve their capability. Ideally, each project or assignment will allow some scope for this.

Functional leaders should have a clear responsibility for staff development. This might include knowledge sharing systems and processes, coaching and organisation of training courses and eLearning opportunities.

> functional leaders should have a clear responsibility for staff development

While retaining responsibility for conducting periodic appraisal interviews, this should be in conjunction with feedback from both the staff member and the cross functional leader(s). Ideally, functional leaders will have regular one-to-one discussions with their functional team members outside of the formal appraisal process.

Communication

This is the key area that both functional and cross functional leaders need to address if cross functional working is to be successful. You will notice that in Figure 8.1 the relationship arrow between these two leaders has a dotted outline, indicating the lack of communication that is most prevalent.

While both types of leader might have regular communication with their team members, it is imperative that they also have regular communication with each other. This should include discussion of staff development issues alongside performance and motivation feedback. As far as the impact on the staff member is concerned, they are effectively fulfilling the role of a single leader but this role is split between two (or more) leaders.

Cross functional working will only deliver effectively over the long term if there is a good channel of communication between all the leaders involved in managing the staff member. Inevitably, there will be conflicting objectives from time to time, but both parties need to be sensitive to these potential conflicts and discuss them openly in order to get performance from the staff member in the short term as well as improving their capability in the longer term.

Ownership

The staff member should be encouraged to take a high degree of ownership for their own performance and development. They should be encouraged to collect evidence that supports their performance achievements, and they should also be encouraged to seek out appropriate development opportunities and keep a record of their progress.

To do this, their performance and development expectations must be clear and agreed. Additionally, the issue of taking ownership for their own performance and development should be made clear and channels of support provided if they encounter any barriers.

On the bench

This process can solve many of the conflicts that arise with cross functional working. In between projects or assignments, staff members are said to be 'on the bench'. During this period they have an opportunity to pursue development activities while preparing or applying for their next assignment. This can include eLearning, training courses, workshops and seminars.

This process works brilliantly if there is, say, a week or two between assignments. It works less well if there is an extended period. How will they practise what they have learned? How will they fill their time productively? What effect will this have on motivation? The process also fails if there is no time at all between assignments because there is little capacity for pursuing development activities.

how will they practise what they have learned?

Cross functional leaders also have to be prepared to take staff onto their projects who are only partially competent in some areas. As we saw in Chapter 3, nobody can become completely competent without applying what they have learned in practical situations.

Clearly, making the 'on the bench' process work requires a high level of planning and co-ordination between functional and cross functional leaders as well as individual staff members.

▶ brilliant example

Sarah was a functional leader with a team of 12 technical specialists under her span of control. She had previously found it difficult to get her staff released from project work to attend training courses and participate in other development activities, but since her company had introduced an 'on the bench' system things had become much better.

As long as she planned ahead, Sarah could normally arrange most training courses and development activities to coincide with her staff being on the bench. It meant that she had to know in advance what their project end dates would be and sometimes she had to influence these dates to ensure that several team members were on the bench at the same time. This enabled courses to be run in-house, which was more cost efficient than sending them on public courses one at a time. Sarah also found that when several team members were on the bench at the same time she could set up knowledge sharing events and also spend time coaching several staff members simultaneously.

Competency analysis

For cross functional structures to work effectively, there needs to be the right level of the right competencies both now and in the future. This requires that senior leaders communicate their forward vision some two or three years ahead so that the right development activities can take place now. It is then for the functional leaders to take a proactive role in ensuring that staff development is aligned with the forward vision so that the right competencies are available as and when required.

It is vital that each functional leader maintains an accurate competency matrix and that these are collated across the organisation. As discussed previously in this chapter, cross functional leaders need to have some scope for supporting development of existing staff, otherwise the organisation will not have the right skills available when they are required. This would result in the expense of having to hire in the right skills as well as making staff redundant if they do not have the required skills.

In short, day-to-day performance cannot be exclusive of longer-term development. This issue is more prevalent with cross functional working and leaders at all levels have to ensure the right balance is struck.

Summary

Cross functional working has the capacity to deliver the flexible and efficient use of human resources. This is particularly true in larger organisations and those with a technology focus. This method of deploying staff to work on projects and assignments, drawn from a pool of functional expertise, gives rise to an eternal triangle consisting of the functional leader, the cross functional leader and the staff member.

This eternal triangle creates some challenges that are centred around communication and conflicting priorities. The main conflict is that the functional leader is focused on staff development while the cross functional leader is focused on day-to-day performance. Resolving these challenges is not easy but there is a series of potential solutions, such as having clear roles and responsibilities, good communication among the two types of leader, a higher level of ownership for both performance and development being taken on by the staff members, utilising a process of 'on the bench' to support staff development and ensuring that staff capability is consistent with the direction of the organisation.

In short, if cross functional working is truly to deliver the benefits of more flexible and efficient human resources, leaders at all levels must rise to the challenges that are presented.

CHAPTER 9

Managing change

A part from death and taxes, change is the one certainty in life. And yet it is an area that has the potential to cause leaders a great many problems. Primarily, these problems come through the resistance to change that many people will have, but also change presents the challenge of ensuring that the situation after the change is better than it was before.

Whether focusing on change within your own discrete team or across a broader organisational horizon, the ability to successfully manage change is another hallmark of becoming a brilliant leader.

Why change?

Change for the sake of change makes no sense. It is not merely enough for you as the leader to know why change is necessary. Your people are more likely to accept change and help you implement it if they understand the reason why change is necessary. There are broadly three reasons for change.

To solve a problem

Problems or issues arise within every business. Sometimes these are due to external factors such as competition, regulation or environmental issues. Other times they are the result of internal factors such as organisational objectives, growth or systems failure. In all cases it is important to get to the root of the issue and identify the underlying problem. Solutions that merely address the symptoms rather than the problem itself will not be long lasting and will give rise to further disruption that could have been avoided.

To improve the status quo

The quest for continuous improvement is to be encouraged. The most common area where you can affect this is likely to be around process improvement, constantly seeking improved efficiency and quality through automation, standardisation and streamlining. Developing staff so that they are capable of more, cross training and knowledge sharing are also likely to improve the status quo. At the organisational level, new technologies and the efficient allocation of resources are likely to be key drivers for improving the status quo.

To exploit an opportunity

Opportunities arise through many avenues. At the organisational level these could be market conditions, the demise of a competitor, new technology or macro factors such as new legislation, economic or political factors. Of course, many of these could be problems rather than opportunities but they are often two sides of the same coin. The leadership skill is to turn problems into opportunities.

> opportunities arise through many avenues

The stakeholders

Who is going to be affected by the change and who needs to contribute to the change being introduced successfully? These are the stakeholders and they need to be engaged in the change process at the earliest opportunity. Small changes might only affect one or two individuals whereas larger changes might affect several teams or even the whole organisation.

While there might be certain issues of confidentiality that prevent engaging people in the change process from the beginning, the earlier they are involved, the better. When people are part of the change process, they take a degree of ownership of it and are more likely to accept the final solution. When change is simply imposed on people, they are more likely to resist it.

The other point you should note here is that leaders do not have a monopoly on the best ideas. Great ideas can come from anyone within the team or organisation. Your role as the leader is to encourage people to make suggestions, assess their ideas and make a decision about the best way forward.

The 10 steps of change

If you aspire to be a good manager of change, the following ten-step process will stand you in good stead.

1 Specify reason/need for change

In order to accept change, people need to understand the reason(s) for it. Ideally, you will be able to highlight the benefits for the organisation, the team and/or the individual. Sometimes there will be conflict among these. For example, a change that benefits the organisation might not be great for the individual. Nonetheless, whether or not there is a personal benefit to the individual, your people need to understand the reason or need for it. This is a primary principle of shared leadership – open communication. The more compelling the reason(s) for change, the more likely you are to gain full acceptance from your people.

2 State the parameters

Alongside the reason(s) for change are the parameters under which your people need to operate. In particular, you need to specify what they can affect within the change parameters and what should be left alone.

▶ brilliant example

Peter runs a call centre team and has been told by senior management that existing processes do not adhere to the new data protection rules. Peter's task is to change the processes so that they are compliant. How should he go about this?

Firstly, he should brief his team on the reason why existing processes need to change. Compliance with the law is a compelling reason to change. Next, he should explain which processes are non-compliant and why.

Peter could simply impose new processes on his team but, given that they operate these processes on a day-to-day basis, it would be better to involve them in suggesting changes. In order to do this, they need to know what the parameters are. Which processes need to change and which ones need to be left alone? What criteria do the new processes need to satisfy in terms of legal compliance, team efficiency and customer satisfaction?

Once the parameters have been explained Peter can encourage his team to come up with suggestions. He decided to do this by forming a working group to address the issue.

3 Encourage participation within the parameters

Once you have made the parameters clear to your team, you should invite their participation based on what they can affect. The more that people are involved in influencing change, the more they will own it and, therefore, the more likely they are to accept the change when it is introduced. When there is major change, as in the preceding example, it is often a good idea to set up a working group within your team to address the change. Those not involved in the working group must not be excluded: their suggestions should still be

> those not involved in the working group must not be excluded

captured and they should be updated on progress along the way.

By turning the change issue into a project like this, it is broadly accepted into the team's psyche even before the final change is announced and implemented. For minor changes, a working group is not necessary but it is still good to invite suggestions and ideas from team members in order to involve them in the change process.

4 Explore ideas and options

Whether inviting suggestions directly to you or via a working group, all relevant ideas and options should be explored. Do they satisfy the change parameters? Are they feasible? What are the pros and cons in relation to the other ideas and options?

5 Decide on the best route

This is a key area where brilliant leaders earn their crust. You have involved your people in the process and you have encouraged them to make suggestions. As stated earlier, you do not have to have a monopoly on the best ideas but what you do need to do is assess those ideas put forward and decide on the best course of action.

To make the right decision you should have key criteria to help you make an objective choice. In our earlier example, the criteria were legal compliance, impact on efficiency and impact on customer satisfaction. The first criterion is non-negotiable: any idea that does not satisfy the legal compliance issue (i.e. the primary reason for change) should be discarded. Of those ideas that are left, which ones are most efficient and have a positive impact on customer satisfaction?

While much of the groundwork can be done by a working group, and while they can present you with a shortlist or recommendation, major change decisions need to be made by you, the leader.

For minor changes you might decide to empower your team to make decisions on your behalf. When you do this, remember that you are still responsible for the changes that are made as it was your decision to empower your team.

6 Gain acceptance from your team and key stakeholders

Once you have made your decision, the next step is to gain acceptance from your team and other key stakeholders who might be affected by the change. Of course, you might also have engaged these key stakeholders earlier in the process, just as you did with your own team.

Communicating your decision at this point requires a degree of influence and persuasion. The first part of the message is to recap on why the change is necessary and the process you have gone through to explore relevant options. You then need to explain your decided course of action. This explanation should include why it is the right choice, the benefits that will be gained and when you propose to implement the change. You should then ask for feedback, including any potential problems that might occur during implementation – these problems need to be addressed prior to implementation.

Your final challenge is to gain acceptance. Ideally, this will be a willing acceptance based on how you have reached your decision and the benefits to the organisation, the team and/or the individual. If you are receiving any resistance at this point you should try to overcome it through persuasion. However, you might need to use position power, as a last resort, in order to force the change through.

7 Implement

Having decided on the best course of action and gained the acceptance of your team and any other key stakeholders, the next step is to implement the changes that have been agreed.

This requires an action plan (which, incidentally, might have been agreed as part of the previous step). As with any action plan, it needs to include a series of connected actions and responsibility allocated to each action along with a deadline.

Your task is then to ensure that each person or group deliver their agreed actions within the deadline. This is the same as managing any other performance expectation.

8 Resolve conflict/resistance

During or shortly after implementation you might experience some conflict among the team or resistance from individuals. Major change sometimes causes conflict because it will temporarily take the team back to the *storming* stage, as discussed in Chapter 6. This is not a bad thing but you do need to address the conflicts in order to take the team beyond the storming stage as quickly as possible.

Resistance can be harder to deal with. Open resistance is unlikely if you have engaged team members in the change process but passive resistance is an altogether different proposition. This is where team members have openly accepted the change but where they are not really happy about it or not really motivated by the situation post change.

> resistance can be harder to deal with

You have two choices with passive resistance. The first is to ignore it and hope that it will disappear eventually. The second is to challenge it and turn it into open resistance. Once it is out in the open you can deal with it, either by persuasion and influence or by using the 'just get on with it' message of position power.

Brilliant leaders will usually opt to draw the resistance out into the open and deal with it through persuasion and influence, sometimes making minor adjustments in order to accommodate individual issues and concerns.

9 Hold the gains

This is an area that is often overlooked in change management. The benefits and payback from changes are not always instant. You have to allow time for the change to be accepted as the norm and for people to realise that the situation post change is better than it was before. You and your team should experience these benefits before making further changes.

During this time you should monitor the situation and collect data to confirm that the changes are working. If the data suggest otherwise, you should use this as an indicator to see why the changes might not be working. But don't be too hasty to make adjustments – it might just need time for the changes to take effect.

On the other hand, if you have made a bad decision you need to acknowledge it and act accordingly to put things right. This will often mean starting from the beginning of the change process. Other times, it might mean that a few simple adjustments are all that are required.

▶ brilliant example

Let's revisit our call centre example.

A working group was formed to review existing processes and make them compliant with data protection legislation. Their secondary objectives were for these processes also to improve efficiency and customer satisfaction.

Peter made the final decision to implement two new processes. The first addressed a series of security checks that needed to be made when answering calls from customers and the second addressed call volumes and answering times. One month after the changes had been implemented the data protection issue had been resolved, more calls were being answered and calls were being answered quicker, but there were an increasing number of customer complaints.

On analysis of these customer complaints it was discovered that customers felt their enquiries were being rushed and that there was a lack of empathy, particularly at the beginning of the calls.

What should Peter do in this situation? Are the new processes failing?

On the surface it would appear that the calls are now legally compliant and efficiency has increased but at the cost of customer satisfaction. There does not appear to be a problem with the new processes per se, but rather the problem appears to be with how the staff are interpreting or working with the new processes. Peter needs to get to the root of this issue and identify whether there is a motivation issue, an interpretation issue and/or a training requirement.

He needs to do this and successfully address the issues before considering any further process changes.

10 Seek further improvements

Once the gains or benefits of change have been firmly established, you should consider any further improvements that can be made. This might mean making minor improvements to the new changes that have been introduced or it might involve more significant change based on other areas where improvement can be made. And this takes us back to our three core reasons for changing in the first place: to solve a problem, to improve the status quo or to exploit an opportunity.

> consider any further improvements that can be made

The culture of change

Many leaders encounter difficulties with introducing and managing change because they do so only when they need to react to a problem or an issue. When there is not a problem or an issue to be solved, they are happy simply to maintain a *norming* team, as discussed in Chapter 6.

Brilliant leaders are not satisfied with merely maintaining the status quo and settling for running a norming team. You should aspire to run a high-performing team. This means that you should make continuous improvement part of your team's culture. In other words, change should be the norm rather than the exception.

In the early days of building a team you should have a focus on knowledge sharing among team members, and as the team matures you should develop this into cross training, encouraging them to question the way things are done. The natural progression is to challenge your team continuously to suggest improvements and involving them in the process of change as much as possible.

When change is accepted as the norm within a working environment, managing change becomes much less problematic than when it is the exception. And when change is proactive and people are involved with it, they are more likely to embrace it rather than resist it.

Summary

There are three main reasons for change: to solve a problem, improve the status quo or exploit an opportunity. The people who are affected by a change and who need to contribute to successful implementation are the stakeholders and these could be from within your team and/or other parts of the organisation. Stakeholders should be involved in the change process at the earliest opportunity.

There is a 10-step process for introducing change.

1 Specify reason/need for change.

2 State the parameters.

3 Encourage participation within the parameters.

4 Explore ideas and options.

5 Decide on the best route.

6 Gain acceptance from your team and key stakeholders.

7 Implement.

8 Resolve conflict/resistance.

9 Hold the gains.

10 Seek further improvements.

Brilliant leaders do not just address change reactively. They make it part of their team's culture by challenging existing norms and continuously seeking to improve.

Further reading

Johnson, Spencer (1998) *Who Moved My Cheese?* Penguin Putnam

Spencer Johnson's world-renowned parody is a light-hearted read with a serious underlying message around the psychology of change. Many leaders have found it to be a useful anecdote in supporting others through the process of change.

CHAPTER 10

Leading without direct reports

n many respects, leading without direct reports is pure leadership. When you don't have the ability to use position power as a way of getting things done, your only option is to use respect power; in other words, you have to use influence to achieve your goals. You have to get people to follow you because they want to and because they buy in to what you are trying to action or achieve, even if you do not manage anyone or direct a team.

> you have to get people to follow you because they want to

So how do you go about leading without the authority of having direct reports?

Primarily, it is about managing relationships effectively, which encompasses networking, being politically savvy and skilful communication. But it is also about building a personal brand for yourself so that others see you in the way that you would like to be perceived. For example, you might like to be seen as a visionary, as an innovator, as a galvanising force within a team or as somebody who consistently gets things done on budget and on time. By building your personal brand, people will begin to see you as a leader, regardless of how much authority you have.

 **tip**

If you want to be seen as a leader, you need to act like a leader. This can be accomplished in any number of ways, such as assuming authority, using 'we' instead of 'I' in your messaging, showing that you care about the success of others and so on.

Building and managing relationships

A good friend of mine is fond of saying that his whole working life revolves around having effective and meaningful conversations. He has only a small team of direct reports but is seen within his organisation as a key leader, which comes from his skill at building and managing relationships.

Networking

You are probably familiar with the expression 'It's not what you know but who you know' – and this is very true when it comes to leading without having direct reports. The level of influence you can command is only likely to be as good as the strength of your network. Do you spend all day with your head down processing tasks or do you take time out to build relationships with people?

This could be as simple as engaging in coffee-machine conversations or attending company social events, through to more meaningful engagements such as making keynote presentations (with follow-up conversations), offering support at inter-departmental meetings and setting up meetings to understand the direction in which other functions are headed.

Political savvy

Building a network is one thing but doing so in a politically savvy way adds another dimension. You need to learn who the key stakeholders are in your organisation, especially in relation to your own functional area and other functions that you need to interact with. Who influences who? Where is there animosity? Where are the landmines? Who do people respect or defer to?

learn who the key stakeholders are in your organisation

The more you can build intelligence around the internal politics within your organisation, the more you can plan your approach accordingly in order to influence others and achieve your goals.

brilliant example

Sandra and James were dependant on each other to deliver a joint plan to improve customer satisfaction via a technology upgrade. As head of a key customer services department, Sandra owned (and had committed to) improving customer satisfaction levels through improved turnaround times that would be enabled by the technology upgrade. James was responsible for purchasing and implementing the technology upgrade.

Despite several meetings, James was dragging his heels and putting a variety of roadblocks in the way of this project. In meetings between the two of them James would agree with actions to move the project along, but outside these meetings he would find reasons not to move these actions forward.

Sandra was very frustrated because one of her own goals, and therefore her bonus, was dependent on this project. Not wishing to be seen as a trouble maker or to damage her relationship with James by escalating the matter, Sandra sought to learn more about how to deal with him. By speaking with others who had worked with James on similar co-dependent projects she discovered that he had negotiated a service contract poorly about a year previously – a mistake that had nearly cost him his job. Ever since, he had been reluctant to make major purchasing decisions.

At their next project meeting, Sandra invited Marlo, a purchasing specialist, to provide input on how to handle negotiations with the supplier. At this ▶

meeting Marlo also agreed to provide ongoing support throughout the negotiations, along with some contractual suggestions about how James could safeguard the organisation's interests. As a result of this intervention, James became more co-operative and the project was able to be completed on time and within budget.

Skilful communication

There is a school of thought that says true leadership is all about skilful communication. While I don't completely buy into this, I do believe it is a critical component and is why I have devoted a complete chapter (Chapter 7) to this area. When you are trying to lead without the authority that comes with direct reports, skilful communication becomes even more important. The key elements to consider are as follows.

Empathy

As Stephen Covey would say, 'Seek first to understand then to be understood.' The ability to demonstrate an understanding of the other person – their needs, their motivations, their fears – will make them more willing to understand the situation from your point of view. As an influencing technique, you should aim to understand the other person's agenda before you can position your agenda in a way that is aligned and, therefore, well received.

Matching communication styles

You will be able to build a better rapport with people if you can match their style when communicating with them. For example, if someone is clearly busy and speaking directly, make sure you get to the point quickly. Similarly, if you are dealing with someone who is analytical, make sure you give them the background and include all relevant facts in order to make your point. A more detailed breakdown of how you can identify people's styles can be found in Chapter 6.

Benefits

When I started in my current role in organisation effectiveness, I had a meeting with the vice president of sales in Europe. His opening line was, 'Tell me about your role and what you can do for me and my team.' This pretty much sums up a really important point when you are trying to influence anyone, but in particular senior managers. People are primarily interested in the benefits you can offer them. If you can clearly answer the question (whether it is asked or not), 'What's in it for me?', you are well on the way to gaining their agreement and support.

Commitment

When you are trying to influence other people in your organisation, you should always aim to conclude the conversation by gaining a commitment to the next steps. A clear action plan that everyone agrees to is a key tool in getting things done, and as such you should regard it as a critical technique in leading without direct reports.

brilliant tip

A great way of wrapping up a conversation when you have summarised the action plan is to ask, 'Is there anything else you need from me?' This provides an opportunity to do two things: firstly, to identify that they are happy with the conversation so far and, secondly, to raise any other issues that they might have.

Building your leadership brand

If you want to be seen as a leader, you have to act like a leader. This is not a one-off activity but involves turning yourself into a brand that represents how you would like others to perceive you.

For example, do you want to be seen as an innovator, a creative force, a go-to person, an expert or a visionary?

brilliant example

Marc was a manager who had a reputation for running a team that consistently delivered excellent results. But he was internally focused and whenever he communicated with people outside his team, the communication was always about making sure his team had what they needed to deliver results. Many of these communications were seen as being an 'Us versus Them' situation – a negotiation rather than a collaboration. As a result, Marc was not seen as a leader by others within the business and this made people question whether he had the right credentials to become a senior manager. In order to convince them otherwise, Marc had to go about reinventing his leadership brand.

The idea of creating a leadership brand is one thing, but the practicality of doing so is altogether more challenging – especially if you are starting from a position that involves previous baggage. That is, do people already have a perception of you that is different from how you would like them to perceive you in the future?

Brand vision and mission statement

The starting point for building your leadership brand is to have a clear vision of how you would like to be perceived by others. From this you can create a mission statement that lays out clearly what you want your leadership brand to be.

 **example**

Marc wanted to be seen as a genuine leader capable of taking on senior management responsibility. This was his vision. He developed the following mission statement: 'To be perceived as a key leader within the organisation, delivering results through my own team and supporting the efforts of others towards the delivery of broader organisational goals.'

From this example, it is clear that Marc identified the aim to continue delivering results while also being seen as a leader in the wider organisational context by supporting the efforts of others. So far so good, but simply making a statement of intent will not ensure that it happens. Two further critical steps are required: communicating this intent and delivering on the promises that it implies.

Marketing yourself

In this context, marketing yourself is about increasing the visibility of your leadership brand, primarily through internal communication. This can be accomplished via a variety of activities, such as:

- presenting at significant company meetings
- attending inter-functional meetings and offering to support other functions' initiatives
- creating initiatives and leading cross functional groups
- lobbying for initiatives that are consistent with your leadership brand or enable you to demonstrate your leadership brand to a wider audience
- publishing white papers and other internal documents that provide visibility of the work you are doing, especially if this is in collaboration with others

- providing support to other functions that enable you to demonstrate your commitment to wider organisational goals
- attending external events and sharing information from these events with people who might find it useful.

This is by no means an exhaustive list of activities but I hope it makes the point that marketing yourself as a leader involves pro-active internal communication. Ideally, this will not be a random set of actions but rather you will plan these activities in advance and then execute them.

▶ brilliant example

In order for Marc to deliver on his stated mission to be perceived as a key leader within the organisation, he needed to market his brand and also be seen to be actively supporting the efforts of others. In addition to delivering results through his own team, Marc set about increasing the visibility of his leadership brand by undertaking a number of new initiatives. These included making an increased number of internal presentations and being more supportive at cross functional meetings. But his biggest success came by creating an initiative to lead a cross functional group that would enable increased service levels to be delivered to the company's top 50 customers. Not only did this help improve his own visibility with senior management but it also helped him to be seen as a leader by his peers, while contributing to the company's goal of increasing customer satisfaction and growing their key accounts.

Live the brand

Ultimately, your leadership brand will succeed or fail based on the actions you take. Are you leading by example? Are you doing things that reinforce and build your leadership brand, or are you doing things that contradict and therefore weaken your brand? Are you visible? Are you seen as being influential? Are you leading groups and projects that deliver results?

you are what you are perceived by others to be

These are all factors that support and reinforce your leadership brand. In short, you are what you are perceived by others to be, and it is this perception that enables you to be seen as a leader and get things done with and through other people, whether they are your direct reports or not.

One final area to consider is that of trust. Can people really trust you? There are a number of ways in which you can inspire trust in others, such as:

- supporting colleagues when they need help or are in trouble
- giving people credit for their input
- recognising the efforts of others and providing them with constructive feedback
- resolving conflicts in a professional and helpful way.

These are all elements that help to build trust between you and others, and are all symptomatic of how you go about building and living your leadership brand.

brilliant tip

If you are engaging in projects with people from other departments and functions, one of the most powerful things you can do to build a sense of collective identity is to unify people around a common vision, aims and goals. If people have a common purpose, they will feel that they are part of the same team, albeit a virtual team that might only be working together temporarily or for a single project.

▶

The fact that you have enabled the creation of this sense of collective identity will mean that the groups see you as a genuine leader.

Summary

Leading without direct reports means that you have to build and use respect power to get things done rather than the authority power that is the default operating style of many managers. In many respects, this can be regarded as *pure leadership*.

Being successful in this area can be broken down into two distinct areas: building and managing relationships; and building your leadership brand. The former involves building an effective network and leveraging these relationships through effective communication while being politically savvy. The latter requires you to be proactive in identifying how you would like others to perceive you and then building a brand around those values. That is, you should have a clear focus via a leadership vision and mission statement, market your brand via a variety of internal communication opportunities and live your brand through the values you exhibit and the actions you take.

By building skill in these two areas you enable yourself to be seen as a leader by others, whether or not they report to you. People will do what you ask them to do because they trust and respect you. People will support you because they want to be part of your success. And most importantly, people will be willing and motivated to be led by you.

Further reading

Covey, Stephen (1989) *The 7 Habits of Highly Effective People*, Simon and Schuster

I believe that Stephen Covey's *The 7 Habits of Highly Effective People* is the definitive text on pure leadership. Its principles can be applied at all times but none more so than in situations where we are leading without having direct reports.

CHAPTER 11

The big picture

hether you are leading a team, a division (several teams) or an organisation (several divisions), you need to have some level of strategic focus in order to get the best out of your people. Both you and they need to understand the bigger picture and how their efforts fit within it. This then is the final piece of the jigsaw in becoming a brilliant leader.

Virtually every aspect of strategic focus covered in this chapter should be regarded as a leadership 'C' task, as discussed in Chapter 5. It is not merely enough to think about these strategic matters but you must also find time to work on them so that your staff get the direction they need.

Points of energy

Notionally a leader has 100 points of energy representing 100 per cent of their time and effort. Are you applying your energy in the right areas? Figure 11.1 overleaf is a simple quadrant model that identifies the four key strategic areas into which you should be exerting your energy, ideally in equal proportion.

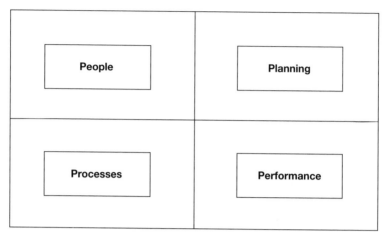

Figure 11.1 Strategic points of energy

Overview

Ultimately, everything a leader does or doesn't do will show up in the form of performance. However, there is a danger that some leaders will put their energy into performance at the expense of the other three key strategic areas – people, planning and processes. This is a very short-term approach to leadership, and brilliant leaders know that they should put their energy into all four areas so that their people are not only performing today but are also positioned to deliver excellent results in the future.

brilliant leaders know that they should put their energy into all four areas

The four areas are not mutually exclusive. In many instances there will be overlap between them. For example, staff development ostensibly falls within the people quadrant. However, staff development should also be planned and there should be good processes in place to support it.

↗ brilliant activity

Try to analyse a typical week in terms of what you spend your time doing. Are you spending a roughly equal amount of time on each of the four leadership Ps or are you spending a disproportionate amount of time on just one or two of them?

If you haven't yet found the right balance, what can you do to shift your energy?

People

There are several ways that you can invest in your people in order to deliver excellent results both now and in the future. Much of this has already been covered throughout this book. Your key energy in this area should include recruiting the right people into your team/organisation (Chapter 2), developing your people (Chapter 3), building team synergy (Chapter 6) and motivation (Chapter 4).

Recruiting the best

Strategically, you shouldn't focus just on what people your team/ organisation might need right now but also on what is likely to be required in the future. This might mean recruiting people with the right skills, but mainly you should be concerned with recruiting people who have the talent to grow and adapt as the team/organisation develops.

Developing your people

This is a key area to which you should apply your energy. By putting effort into developing your people now, they will be capable of delivering better results in the future. The main tools at your disposal are training courses, coaching/mentoring and targeted job assignments (leap experiences). You can have a positive effect on enabling the development of your people whether you are leading at the team, divisional or organisational level. This can be through direct facilitation or by creating a culture in which it can happen, together with an appropriate budget allocation.

Building team synergy

There are many ways a leader can help to build team synergy but, in particular, your focus should be on cross training, knowledge sharing and taking your team(s) effectively through the various stages of their development. This is an area that is primarily the domain of each individual team leader.

Motivation

There are many factors that potentially motivate or demotivate staff members, as discussed in Chapter 4. Your challenge is to identify what those factors are for your people and try to enable them wherever possible as well as minimising the occurrence of demotivating factors. At the individual or team level this is quite straightforward as you will be close to your team members. When considering motivation from a divisional or organisational level this becomes more challenging as you have to try to affect the majority of the most common motivational factors or, as a minimum, allow team leaders as much freedom as possible to do so.

Planning

failing to plan is
planning to fail

Failing to plan is planning to fail and brilliant leaders know this. Leaders at all levels should spend a lot of their energy planning so that their teams can operate proactively and in an organised manner.

There are lots of areas where planning is important and the following are by no means exhaustive.

Resources

What will your team need in order to produce excellent results? This could be planning the right human and/or physical resources such as equipment. It is often counter productive to try to obtain the right resources reactively and, wherever possible, they should be planned in advance so that they are in place when needed.

Change

Sometimes you will have to instigate change reactively, usually to solve a problem that has occurred. Ideally, as discussed in Chapter 9, change will be proactive. This requires that you identify change situations or opportunities in advance and plan for them.

Budgets

In most organisations, managers are compelled to produce budgets as an annual event but proper budgetary planning goes beyond this. What are the plans for your team(s)? What is the cost versus benefit of these plans? Do you need to lobby for funds based on this cost/benefit analysis?

Training and staff development

Some staff development is driven by short-term operational requirements. Ideally, though, much of it will be planned in advance based on a training needs analysis of your team(s). This analysis should take account of the existing competency levels of team members and the areas that require development for the team to meet future performance requirements. The actual plan should focus on the most effective and efficient methods of developing staff, as discussed in Chapter 3.

Projects

Aside from the day-to-day work of your team there will be the opportunity for specific projects that enable the team to progress and excel. These projects might be based on improvements (e.g. processes), stretch objectives (i.e. exceptional performance) or special assignments aimed at developing staff members or exploring new opportunities. Ideally, you will be able to plan these projects in advance and build them into the workflows and performance expectations of your team.

Processes

In Chapter 9 we considered how change is best handled if team members are engaged in the process. Strategically, it is much better if change is handled proactively rather than reactively. While there are many aspects of change, the one area where there is nearly always an opportunity for improvement surrounds processes within your team. This might include automation, efficiency improvements or increased effectiveness.

There are essentially two approaches open to you. Firstly, you can identify areas for improvement and challenge your team to work on these areas under your guidance. This can take the form of targeted projects. Alternatively, you can encourage your team to identify areas for improvement and then allow them to develop these improvements. Which route you take is likely to depend on the stage of development your team is at, as discussed in Chapter 6. The more mature your team is, the more independence you should try to give them.

▶ brilliant example

Jackie had been leading her risk management team for over three years and they had consistently delivered good results. Every team member was competent in their own roles and also able to cover each other's roles during periods of leave or absence.

During a recent review meeting with her new boss, Jackie was surprised to receive feedback that she should try to take her team to new heights, after all they were delivering exactly what was required of them. Her boss explained that while they were delivering a consistently good performance, there had been little improvement in their output for over a year.

Jackie was encouraged to challenge her team to identify process improvements that might deliver better results. To her surprise, they actually had several really useful ideas, most of which Jackie was happy to support. After several months, the team had implemented the new processes and were performing at a much higher level.

Performance

The three previous Ps in our quadrant all contribute to long-term performance. But, of course, you must also be concerned with short-term performance and a balanced proportion of your energy should be spent in this area. Ensuring performance expectations are made clear to team members, monitoring performance and providing feedback on progress are all elements you should focus on, as discussed in Chapter 4.

> you must also be concerned with short-term performance

The challenge faced by most leaders is to avoid spending a disproportionate amount of their energy in this area to the detriment of the other three. This is the sort of short-term approach that creates a reactive working environment where one crisis is followed by another. The balance you need to find is spending enough time and effort on short-term performance while also investing energy in future performance so that your results are sustainable over the longer term.

Environment

I made the point in the Introduction to this book that brilliant leaders create an environment in which people can perform to a high level. Much of what has been covered in the preceding chapters will enable you to create such an environment. However, as I bring this book to a close, there are two further areas that I would encourage you to consider when creating an environment in which your people can thrive.

Lead by example

No doubt you have heard this expression many times before but it really is very important if you are to earn the respect of your team members. If you want them to be committed to self-development, you must also be committed yourself. If you want them to share their knowledge, you must be prepared to too. If you want them to work proactively, so must you. And so on.

Every aspect of how you want your staff to behave must be mirrored in the way you behave yourself. If you adopt a 'do as I say, not as I do' approach to managing your people, you will be using position power rather than the all important respect power adopted by brilliant leaders.

Culture

Perhaps one of the most powerful things you can do to create a brilliant team environment is to develop the right culture within your team. Culture is created by vision, values and working methodologies and, as the leader, you are in an ideal position to positively affect all three.

Communicate your vision for the team often so that it is in their psyche. While you can influence the team's values, the values should not just come from you. People are more likely to adhere to a set of values if they have a role in developing them. They are not just something that can be discussed theoretically at a team meeting. You can also influence the team's values by recognising and praising the actions of team members as well as listening to those things that are important to them.

Working methodologies are something that you will directly influence in the early stages of the team's development, but as the team matures you should encourage them to develop and improve those methodologies. Again, if they have a role in influencing the way they work, team members are more likely to take ownership of their own environment and contribute to a team culture in which they can thrive.

Summary

A leader notionally has 100 points of energy, representing 100 per cent of their time and effort. You should aim to exert 25 points of energy in each of the four key strategic areas:

> aim to exert 25 points of energy in each of the four key strategic areas

people, planning, processes and performance. The shortcoming of many leaders is that they spend a disproportionate amount of time focusing on short-term performance to the detriment of factors that will enable their team(s) to thrive in the longer term and drive future performance to exceptional levels. Brilliant leaders are able to find the right balance.

Additionally, brilliant leaders are able to create an environment in which people can perform well. Much of the coverage of this book has focused on how such an environment can be created but there are two further areas worthy of your consideration. The first is always to lead by example. The second is to create the right culture within your team by effectively communicating your vision, developing shared values and creating working methodologies that are both effective and owned by your team.

I hope this final chapter has helped you to join together all the others throughout this book so that you can put them into practice and become a brilliant leader. You should not regard them as a set of standalone principles and techniques. Brilliant leadership requires that you mix them together to develop a consistent and integrated approach.

I wish you well in your endeavour.

What did you think of this book?

We're really keen to hear from you about this book, so that we can make our publishing even better.

Please log on to the following website and leave us your feedback.

It will only take a few minutes and your thoughts are invaluable to us.

www.pearsoned.co.uk/bookfeedback

Bibliography

Belbin, Meredith (2004) *Management Teams: Why They Succeed or Fail*, Elsevier Butterworth-Heinemann

Briggs, Katharine and Briggs Myers, Isabel, Myers-Briggs Type Indicator, http://www.myersbriggs.org

Covey, Stephen (1989) *The 7 Habits of Highly Effective People*, Simon and Schuster

Eichinger, Robert, Lombardo, Michael and Stiber, Alex (2005) *Broadband Talent Management: Paths to Improvement*, Lominger International

Geier, John, DiSC Profile System, http://www.discprofile.com

Gratton, Lynda (2007) *Hot Spots: Why Some Companies Buzz with Energy and Innovation – and Others Don't*, Prentice Hall

Honey, Peter and Mumford, Alan, Learning Styles, http://www.peterhoney.com

Johnson, Spencer (1998) *Who Moved My Cheese?* Penguin Putnam

Kolb, David (1984) *Experiential Learning: Experience as the Source of Learning and Development*, FT Press

Landsberg, Max (1996) *The Tao of Coaching*, HarperCollins

Lombardo, Michael and Eichinger, Robert (2004) *FYI For Your Improvement*, Lominger International

Ollander-Krane, Jason and Johnson, Neil (1993) 'Growing by Leaps and Bounds', *The Journal of Human Resource Development*

Patterson, Kerry, Grenny, Joseph, McMillan, Ron and Switzler, Al (2002) *Crucial Conversations: Tools for Talking When Stakes Are High*, McGraw-Hill

Porter, Elias H., Strength Deployment Inventory, http://www.personalstrengths.com

Richardson, Linda (2009) *Sales Coaching*, McGraw-Hill

Tuckman, Bruce (1965) 'Developmental Sequence in Small Groups' (article), http://www.infed.org/thinkers/tuckman.htm

Index